That's Cork

Tom Galvin graduated from University College Dublin and St Patrick's College, Maynooth, before moving to Poland, where he began a career in journalism. He went on to become editor of *In Dublin* magazine and has contributed to *The Irish Times*, the *Sunday Independent*, *Backpacker* and *Abroad* magazines. In 2004 his first book, *The Little Book of Dublin*, was published.

He has also contributed to the *Evening Herald* and *Village* magazine.

That's Cork

Tom Galvin

The Collins Press

Published in 2005 by
The Collins Press
West Link Park
Doughcloyne
Wilton
Cork

© Tom Galvin 2005

Tom Galvin has asserted his moral right to be identified
as author of this work.

British Library Cataloguing in Publication Data

Galvin, Tom
    That's Cork
    1. Cork (Ireland) – History 2. Cork
    (Ire land) – Social life and customs
    I. Title
    941.9' 56

ISBN–1-903464-76-5

Typesetting: The Collins Press

Font: Helvetica, 10 point

Cover design: Design Matters

Printed in Ireland by ColourBooks Ltd.

Contents

It came from the marshes:
a brief history of Cork

Finbarr & the hung-head monks of Cork
Although contemporary scholars are now debating whether he existed at all, the man held responsible for the founding of Cork was Finbarr, meaning 'Fair Crest'; the title referring to his hair, which was said to have been particularly dazzling. The oldest known account of Finbarr's life dates from the twelfth century – several hundred years after his lifetime – and his family background is as colourful as his hair. According to the account, his father, Amairgein Uí Briúin of Connacht, was the offspring of an incestuous relationship between a king and his own daughter. Driven by guilt, the king attempted to kill Amairgein, who survived, but was banished to live in Munster where he was employed as a blacksmith by another king, Tigernach. Tigernach had a female slave who attended to him alone, but Amairgein slept with her

1

and she became pregnant. The enraged king was going to have them both burnt but the story goes that the unborn child 'spoke to him from the womb' and they were spared. The child was born at Garranes, west Cork, around 548 and was christened Lochan but was given the name Finbarr by the monks who educated him. He later set himself up as a hermit at a corrie lake in Gougane Barra, which is the source of the River Lee. Guided by an angel, he moved downriver to the great marsh of Munster, fasted for three days and was given land by a nobleman whereby he founded his church some time around 606. Many miracles are attributed to Finbarr, and the people of Cork are particularly grateful for his greatest one. According to the story, Finbarr was told that when he blessed the church there would be 'an abundance of wisdom continually in Cork'. And there you have it.

Finbarr went to Rome to receive orders from the Pope, Gregory the Great – patron saint of choirboys, singers, the plague and gout among other things – who told him to return to Cork where God would consecrate him as a bishop. This Finbarr did and he became abbot of Cork. A law tract at that time gave abbots the same status as a king in Munster, so Finbarr would have been quite a powerful man. He also established a school that would become a great seat of learning and place Cork on the map internationally, since it was supposedly attended by many Irish saints and European scholars. Before Finbarr died in 623, he expressed a wish to be buried in Cork at the site of the cathedral that he had established, and promised that anybody buried in the cemetery 'would never know the torments of hell'. Word must have got out before the cathedral was fully rebuilt in the late nineteenth century; 17,000 people are registered as being buried there between 1800 and 1850 and the cemetery had to be closed in 1860.

There is a saying in Ireland that the farther north you get, the meaner the people get. Maybe whoever wrote it had a dodgy compass. The earliest existing manuscript from the Cork monastery is a poem called 'Sen Dé' (Blessing of God) written by Colman Moccu Cluasaigh and composed in the year 664 on the occasion of a great plague. The more interesting monastic text relating to Cork monks is called *Aislinge Meic Con Glinne*, *The Vision of Mac Conglinne*. Written about 1050, it describes the unsavoury treatment of a monk visiting from the north. Given nothing but a bowl of oats to eat, cold bath water to wash in and flea-ridden sheets for a bed, he called the monks of Cork curs, robbers and shit-hounds. Or to quote:

ye curs and ye robbers and dunghounds, and unlettered brutes, ye shifting, blundering hung-head monks of Cork.

That's Cork.

An axe to grind – Cork and the Vikings

The abbey and university that had been established in Cork existed for over 250 years until the Vikings arrived in 820. The Vikings, whose list of desirables included the blood of priests and the plunder in the churches, must have found a playground in early monastic Cork. They wreaked havoc in the university and abbey and burned the surrounding city. Eighteen years later they returned again and did likewise. In 846 they came back and finally settled, making a permanent residence where they landed at present-day Barrack Street/Sullivan's Quay. They later established another settlement on one of the islands in the Great Marsh and the natives called it 'Little Cork' to distinguish it from the larger settlement on the southern hill where Finbarr's abbey was situated.

As with the story of Finbarr, much of the knowledge of the Viking period in Cork is sketchy, because written accounts unfortunately do not exist. By the end of the twentieth century only a penny bearing the inscription Anluf Guthfrithsson (939-41) minted at York, and a silver penny giving the name of the legendary Eric Bloodaxe, king of Northumbria (947-9, 952-9) were still the only Viking coins to have been discovered in Cork. However, in February 2004 the 1,000-year-old remains of a rectangular Viking house just off Cork's South Main Street, on the site of the former city car park, and close to the River Lee, were discovered. Doorposts, a threshold beam and a section of wattle wall were clearly visible. Fish bones and scales, weighing-scale measures, fragments of decorated combs, parts of a small Viking boat, metal clothing pins, shoe leather and shards of pottery were also found. The more curious find however, was layers of oyster shells around the site. Apparently these would have been used to line the floors.

Another legacy of the Vikings is poll tax, a tax levied on each individual equally, regardless of status or wealth. Poll tax was the main cause of the Peasants' Revolt in England in 1381 and brought Margaret Thatcher to her knees in 1990. Imposed in Cork in 1012, the tax became known as the 'nose tax' because those who did not pay it had their noses slit.

In a reappraisal of the Viking assaults on sacred buildings, some historians believe it was nothing personal, but simply a method of cutting down on the laborious task of plundering individual homes by raiding what was really the equivalent of the banks – the monasteries. They are reputed to have sacked Cork monastery on about eleven occasions but, on the plus side, they did build the first quaysides in Cork.

The Vikings also contributed to the development of shipbuilding in Ireland by introducing the keel into boat making. A substantial number of words related to shipping derive from Old Norse like bow, keel, skeg, and stern. Viking names in Cork include Skiddy, Coppinger, and Keyser, as in Keyser's Lane near the South Gate Bridge; Keyser means 'a passage leading to the waterfront' and Keyser's Lane, heading to the river, is thought to be the oldest street in Cork.

'Gaelicised' names of Vikings suggest that by the twelfth century they had ceased their plundering and had begun to have better relations with the natives – as in Macalf (son of Olaf) Ua Dubgaill. Dubgaill means 'dark foreigner' which related to hair and not skin and was what the Vikings were called at the time. The name specifically refers to those Vikings who came from Denmark, known as Dubh Ghaill, 'black-haired foreigners', rather than the Vikings from Norway, who were termed Fionn Ghaill 'white-haired foreigners'.

The Stormin' Normans

The Irish name for Cork is Corcaigh, which means 'marsh' and was originally tagged with Mór, meaning 'the great marsh of Munster'. The most important element in the city's development was the River Lee, which splits into two channels just west of the city centre, each channel flowing around the city before meeting again in Cork Harbour. This means that the city centre is an island among a number of islands through which channels of the Lee are threaded. The first island to be developed measured 690 by 240 yards (630 by 220 m approximately) and had one straight street, the Main Street, with a north bridge and a south bridge.

Cork was captured by the Anglo-Normans in 1177 and received its charter somewhere between 1185 and 1189 – a date that is still not resolved but that did not prevent Corkonians celebrating their eight-hundredth birthday in 1995. The name Corcaigh was shortened to Corke when it became a royal town and, from then on, the city enjoyed privileges similar to Bristol. It was the first town in Ireland to have its name anglicised. In 1206 the Castle of Cork was built by the English at the site of the Queen's Old Castle on Grand Parade.

The Anglo-Normans built the city walls and the task of building on the marshy land was a dangerous one. For a cost of £55 and 5s in 1211/12, walls were built five to six m in height and up to 10ft/3 m thick, encompassing an area of about 14.5 hectares (36 acres). Given the nature of the land and the tidal floods, one wonders how they managed foundations. The walls were made of large limestone blocks laid on brushwood and moss on the river mud. Beneath the mud, luckily, there was a natural bed of gravel which acted as a foundation; otherwise, it would have been an impossible task. The walls of Cork were a lot stronger than those in other cities in the country. The walls of Limerick were 7 ft/2m; Kilkenny's were 4.5 ft/1.4m; Athlone's were 3 ft/1m; and the walls at Youghal were only 2 ft/0.6m.

Eighteen towers were built at various points on the walls and access to the city was through two gates at the north bridge and south bridge, giving them their titles, North Gate Bridge and South Gate Bridge. There was a water gate at the spot where the Queen's Old Castle used to be, so ships could pass under it and be berthed inside the city walls. (Later, house sizes would be advertised in 'ship lengths' because of this.) This gives us the city's coat of arms: two battlemented towers with a medieval galleon sailing between them. The Latin motto for Cork reads *Statio Bene Fida Carinis*, which means a 'safe anchorage for ships' and is taken from the second book of Virgil's *Aeneid*. Thankfully some bright spark substituted Virgil's original word, *Male,* for *Bene*, otherwise it would have meant a bad harbour for ships. With the Normans Cork city became something of a fortress.

In 1241, King Henry III issued another charter, which hints at the make up of the populace, the independent nature of the city and a worrying xenophobia:

> And no foreigner may have a wine tavern except on board a ship. And no foreigner may sell cloth in the said city.
>
> And that no foreign merchant may remain in the town with his wares for the purpose of selling the same for more than 40 days, except with the consent of said Citizens.
>
> And no foreign merchant may purchase any Corn, Leather or Wool within the aforesaid City, except from the citizens thereof.

Foreigners at the time would have meant anyone from outside the city and not from overseas.

In 1326, Cork, along with Dublin and Drogheda, became a 'staple' town, which meant that only these three towns had the right to hold the 'staple' or market for hide, wool and woolfells. These became Ireland's chief exports in the fourteenth century, replacing tillage farming after the famines in the early fourteenth century. During that time (1315-17) a series of disastrous harvests and famine threatened the survival of the English colonialists in Cork county, who tried to emigrate in large numbers to England. So great were the numbers leaving that by 1344, no one, apart from merchants, was permitted to leave Ireland without a royal licence. By 1388 the citizens of Cork were also emigrating in vast numbers, despite a royal writ urging them to stay for the 'defence' of the city.

The Anglo-Normans built post-and-wattle and sill-beam houses, the materials of which were highly flammable and, for the first 300 years in the city's history as a walled town, it was illegal to have a fire lighting at night. Heavy fines were imposed for those in breach of the ban and the fine became known in local parlance as 'smoke silver'. On 1 December 1386 a tax of one farthing was laid on every house 'from which smoke issued' – every house with a chimney basically. The money thus levied was used to pay for watchmen to keep an eye both within and without; apart from the dangers of fire, the walls of Cork were under constant attack from the natives.

Cork, the little city state

As with all medieval cities, a town crier was employed to announce any serious news after ringing a bell to gather the citizens. In Cork, the crier assembled the people in the North Main Street opposite the entrance to St Francis' Church. The night watchman also had the job of announcing the more innocuous news as he went about his business; such as the time and weather every hour and reporting that 'all is well', meaning there were no fires or serious attacks. Being woken up to be told things are fine seemed a fairly pointless exercise. But worse apparently, was the state of these criers, who acted as guards before they were done away with some time before 1800.

Cork, for almost 400 years, was essentially a little city state of Cork, an English settlement on the south coast of Ireland almost completely free from outside influences and governed by its town council, bailiffs and a mayor, levying their own taxes and holding their own courts. Perhaps the reason they were so self-sufficient was because they could never go outside the walls without the natives bothering them. Raphael Hollingshead's *Chronicles of England, Scotland and Ireland*, written around 1577, said: 'The Townspeople could not walk outside the walls for recreation without fear of being molested. These people traded, suffered and fought for centuries.' The extent of the citizens' concerns for their safety from outlaws and attack can be witnessed in their payment of a 'black rent' of £40 per annum to Cormac mac Taidgh MacCarthy, Lord of Muskerry, who took possession of Blarney from the Lombards in the 1480s and built the castle with the famous stone. That put him only 8km from the city centre, so the citizens paid him to leave them alone.

The population of medieval Cork has only been guessed at, given the lack of source material. What was discovered, however, was that the average height for men was 170cm (5' 7"); and for women it was 157cm (5' 2"). These measurements were taken from skeletons found at St Mary's of the Isle (near Pope's Quay) where the majority were buried in the medieval times. Less than two per cent of those sampled had lived beyond the age of 50 and virtually all suffered considerable dental wear owing, it is presumed, to the grit in the flour at the time, which was not carefully sifted. They must have eaten a lot of bread. Their fashion sense was pretty brutal too. According to Tuckey's *Remembrancer*, (or, *Annals of the City and County of Cork*), written in 1837, their shoes were so long that their walking was encumbered, so they tied the points of their shoes to their knees – the gentlemen with chains of silver gilt and the women with laces. The custom was in vogue until 1467, when it was actually prohibited, with the threat of a fine for anyone who continued to dress in such a manner.

As for the natives? Richard Stanyhurst, who observed and wrote about the native Irish people in the sixteenth century and also contributed to Hollingshead's *Chronicles of England, Scotland and Ireland*, seems to have discovered the source of the 'mullet', the hairstyle with the long back and short sides, when he had the following to say about the natives in Cork.

> Proud they are of their long crisped bushes of hair, which they term glibs [locks of hair which hang down over the eyes]; and the same they nourish with all their cunning: to crop the front thereof they take it for a notable piece of villainy.

He also observed that they were born fighters.

> They used a damnable superstition, leaving the right arms of their infants unchristened, to the intent that it might give a more ungracious and deadly blow.

The hair was also considered useful in a scrap, because it was recorded that:

> their hands and heads they never wash, cleanse nor cut, especially their heads, the hair whereof they suffer to grow … it groweth so fast together that is instead of a hat, and keepeth the head warm, and also will bear off a great blow or stroke …

Quakers, fools and madmen – Cork expands

In 1641, the population of Cork was estimated at anywhere between about 3,000 and 8,000. However, Sir Richard Cox, governor of Cork in 1691, who founded the town and English settlement at Dunmanway in 1693, estimated the population in 1685 at '20,000 souls'. Even then it was described as – sorry Cork – 'the second best citty of Ireland' and not the first. He also wrote that it:

> is generally inhabited by English and those industrious and rich … The most memorable things recorded in this citty are … The merchant's walk made 1668, the King's Castle reedified, 1670. County court built, 1671. City court built, for £460, 1674. South Bridge built for £285, 1675.

Jonathan Swift, around 1706, recorded:

> There is not an acre in Ireland turned to half its advantage, yet it is better improved than the people, and all those evils are the affects of English misrule, so your sons and grandchildren will find to their sorrow. Cork indeed was a place of trade, but for some years past is gone to decay, and the wretched merchants, instead of being dealers, are peddlers and cheats.

Not alone in his opinions, in a letter to Swift in 1736, Lord Orrery wrote from Cork city:

The butchers are greasy, the Quakers as formal; and the Presbyterians as holy and full of the Lord as ever; all things in *statu quo*; even the hogs and pigs grunt in the same cadence as of yore; unfurnished with variety, and dropping under the natural dullness of the place, materials for a letter are as hard to be found, as money, sense, honesty, or truth.

He finally left the city that year and described how even his horse was dying to get out.

I am going to transplant myself to the pale. Farewell Cork and all its beauties. Adieu ye kennels flowing with bullocks' blood! Adieu ye roaring captives in the North Gate! Quakers, fools and madmen, all Adieu. My sorrowful heart is burst. My horse stands pawing at the door. The last piece of bread and butter is in my mouth; a thousand beggars await me. I come ye limping miscreants, I come.

Now that's Cork.

From about the eighth century a green existed (probably close to the present Evergreen Street) which was part of the ancient *Faithche* or 'green of Cork', a place that was initially intended for games. It had to be actually rented by the citizens from the Crown after the Normans took the city, and it was then enclosed by a stone wall. By medieval times the fun and games had ceased and the green had become 'Gallows Green'. The first recorded hanging, in 1644, of one Viscountess Fermoy, who was hanged for refusing to denounce her Catholic faith. Bodies of the executed were buried in a communal ground on Lapps Island (now the site of Cork Harbour Commissioners) and the heads were put on spikes on the South Gate Prison walls. It got so busy up on the spikes that milk women who passed under the gate on their daily rounds had to place covers on the cans of milk they carried because so much hair was falling from the heads into the milk.

A 'strange but true' tale with a spot of gallows humour. On 10 September 1766 a tailor called Patrick Redmond was executed for robbery at Gallows Green. At least, that was the plan. But in the town at the time was a wandering actor named Glover who restored Redmond to life by 'friction and fumigation' after he had been left for dead having hung for a full nine minutes. Redmond made his escape, got drunk and went to the theatre where Glover was performing that evening, to thank him. The audience, many of whom had seen him hang that day, thought it was the best act they had ever witnessed. Redmond was actually recorded as the third tailor who had made his escape from the gallows that century. Lord knows what the tailors had done, but punishing those for making and selling inferior goods was quite commonplace, with tarring and feathering first performed as a punishment in Cork on 24 August 1784, when a shoemaker was said to have 'made up shoes of an inferior quality at so low a price, as to prove highly injurious to the craft'.

Others resorted to their own methods for dealing with crime. There was a Mr Nixon, a hardware owner, who in 1773 was fed up of being robbed and set a 'gin rat-trap' in his shop. (What were the rats like in those days if gin was the most efficient bait?) The thief caught his fingers in the trap, was captured and was 'whipped three market days'. When the two new prisons were opened in Cork – the County Prison on Western Road in 1791 and the Cork City Prison at Sunday's Well in 1820 – the green was abandoned and flogging and executions stopped. By 1850 the *Faithce* was finally built upon. The last flogging in Cork was in 1820.

Cork is one of the wettest cities in Ireland (anything up to 1,145mm per annum) but according to Tuckey's *Remembrancer*, there were some truly weird goings on in the eighteenth century. In the summer of 1748, in Doneraile, north of Cork city, a shower of 'yellowish substance, which resembled brimstone and had a sulphurous smell fell from the sky'. On 1 May 1753, the greatest and longest shower of hail ever remembered fell. On 1

November 1755 a violent earthquake was felt at 36 minutes past nine in the morning. On 31 March 1761 an earthquake was recorded at Cork and Kinsale for about a minute, after which the tide rose two feet 'and ebbed away in the space of four minutes with great force'. The confused Corkonians, as if the gods had not been entertained enough, on 20 June 1762 'prayed for rain in all churches' after not a drop had fallen for thirteen weeks. On 11 January 1768 the greatest fall of snow for over 40 years was recorded with falls of up to six feet deep. On 24 May 1768 prayers for fair weather were offered up in all the churches. On 14 August 1770 a shower of rain fell in Cork city that was so heavy for three hours that boats were floating on the streets. But no rain fell on the north side. What had the northsiders done to prevent it? Better prayers? On 8 November 1768 a meteor was seen over Cork 'much brighter than the moon and of double its diameter' then, on 30 March the following year a 'ball of fire' fell from the clouds on a cabin near Castletownroche, killing one man – and a pig. Now that's Cork.

The superstitious folk of Cork were again ruffled on 27 March 1784, when an air balloon had been set off from the Mardyke. It drifted to Cooper's Hill, about 16 miles away, where the inhabitants, who had never seen or heard anything like it before, were convinced it was the devil. When the balloon settled between two rocks some men were brave enough to capture it and take it home and soon all the neighbours had gathered round to see 'the Lucifer'. The story goes that someone accidentally dropped a spark on the balloon, whereupon it exploded (clearly full of flammable gas) scorching several of the onlookers. Others fainted and those left standing ran for their lives, convinced that the devil had let loose the flames of hell. On 14 April the same year another balloon was launched in Fleet Street in London and was found in a field at Fair Hill in Cork. There are no reports of anyone approaching that one. The first actual flight in a balloon over Cork took place on 2 September 1816 by James Sadler at 4.40pm and ended at 5.12pm. Sadler was the first to attempt crossing the Irish Sea by balloon. He left Dublin on 1 October 1812 but came down past the Isle of Man unfortunately; luckily it was on top of a herring trawler called *Victory* and he was spared a watery grave.

The Cork Savings Bank opened for business on 20 December 1817. There had been banks in operation before that, but a new law stipulated that money had to be deposited with the government for safekeeping. A meeting was called in the commercial buildings, which are now the Imperial Hotel, and the meeting was attended by the Church of Ireland bishop of Cork and Ross together with the Catholic bishop. In what must have been an historic occasion, both agreed that the bank's workforce was to be voluntary. If a volunteer did not show up for work, he was to be fined five shillings. Now that's Cork.

The population of Cork in 1752 was 41,175. By 1796 it had reached 57,000, and by 1821 it had increased to 71,500. In 1901 Cork's population was 76,122 – not much growth in almost 100 years. In 1823 the death rate in Cork was at 150 per 1,000 births. But the Great Famine of the 1840s decimated the population and between the death tolls and emigration the city felt the effects. In 1846, with the death toll rising rapidly, Cork Workhouse advertised for a burial ground. In the first nine months of 1847, 10,000 people were buried in St Joseph's Cemetery. The guardians attempted to use St John's Graveyard in Douglas Street, but locals stood guard for three nights to prevent any further burials. Eventually, Carr's Hill was used as a paupers' graveyard, the site of which is now a memorial to the victims. The Carr's Hill site continued to be used for the next hundred years to bury paupers. In 1920, it came under the control of the Cork District Board – later the Southern Health Board – and was still in use in the 1940s. In 1950, a Cork taxi driver,

Olaf Sorenson (another Norse connection for Cork), helped financially to erect an illuminated cross 80 feet high here to commemorate the Famine victims and the paupers buried there. The lights went out in the 1980s, partly through lack of funding and partly due to the fact that it was confusing pilots on their descent into Cork airport. In January 2002, the cross was once more illuminated with the assistance of a company based in Ringaskiddy, Novartis.

Despite the Famine in Cork, someone had to make a profit. Cork's Patent Saw Mills had twenty pairs of saws working almost non-stop, cutting wood to make coffins, sheds for temporary fever 'hospitals' and berths for ships carrying emigrants. Other ships still left Cork Harbour with exports, despite the fact that the population was starving. The first 'Soup Kitchen' in Ireland to help the victims of famine was in Barrack Street in Cork and fed 1,300 people daily. With the hinterland of Cork being entirely tillage country, the potato blight had severe effects, with the only other source of food being boiled seaweed; a dish called *dhoola-maun*, which although it had some beneficial properties also caused severe diarrhoea, from which many people died. America sent two warships with food and supplies to help the Famine victims in Cork: the sloop, *Jamestown*, and the frigate,

Macedonian. The former arrived in Cobh on 12 April 1847, the latter on 28 July, met by a welcoming party that included Fr Theobald Mathew, the founder of the Temperance Movement.

Anyone who knows anything about Cork is aware that the city is jinxed when it comes to fires, which makes it baffling as to why it took so long for the fire brigade to come into operation. The 'Great Fire of Cork' occurred in 1622 and over 1,500 houses were destroyed. The cause was put down to lightning, so the corporation banned thatch on houses and ordered all roofs that were made of thatch to be replaced by slate. The methods of dealing with fires at the time were not very elaborate and were more of a hindrance than a help – long poles with iron crooks were used to pull down blazing timbers, which meant sparks could drift on to other rooftops, thus spreading the fire. Fires then came under the remit of insurance companies who, purely with their own interests in mind, hired people to deal with blazes in their properties. The first Cork City Fire Brigade was not formed until 1877, but it took another large fire, the burning of the first courthouse in March 1890, to convince the city to get on with the task of building the first fire station, built on Sullivan's Quay.

The general election of 16 June 1922 was important in many ways. It was contested the same day as the Draft Irish Constitution, the Treaty, was published and it was also the first election to be conducted under the system of proportional representation. Fearing confusion, a poem was published in the *Cork Examiner* on the morning of the election for the benefit of those Corkonians unsure of what to do. It was called 'How to Vote' and went like this:

> Put figure 1 to the name of your favourite
> And 2 to the next you prefer
> Then put 3, 4 and 5 in the way you think right
> Against three of the other names there.

Now that's definitely Cork.

At the end of the last millennium, Cork Corporation buried a time capsule in the city. Amongst other things, they placed in it a Roy Keane jersey alongside a tape of Jack Lynch's graveside oration at the funeral of Christy Ring.

The city works (most of the time)

Amsterdam, Venice, Paris, Cork

Cork vaudeville entertainer, Danny La Rue (born Daniel Patrick Carroll), who prefers the term 'comic in a frock' to 'drag queen', described the city of Cork as the Venice of Ireland. Many visitors down through the years have compared it to Amsterdam, particularly when the city was replete with canals and waterways. And what would Cork people make of the comparisons? There is a joke in which a Corkman says to his mate, 'I was reading in a magazine that they are describing Cork as the Paris of Ireland.' The other replies, 'Why aren't they calling Paris the Cork of France?'

Cork is now home to 123,000 people (225,000 in the greater Cork, or metropolitan area) and is the second largest city in the Republic of Ireland. The city comprises of 3,731 hectares. The average rainfall per year is 1,145mm; most of the east part of Ireland gets between 1,000mm and 1,250mm per year. Cork is twinned with Coventry in England (1969), Rennes in France (1982), San Francisco in USA (1984) and Cologne in Germany (1988). Shanghai, in China (with a population of eighteen million), is the next city to be 'twinned' with Cork.

Cork was designated as the European Capital of Culture for 2005, but the city loses out in the tourist market, attracting only ten per cent of the 2.6 million visitors to the Cork-Kerry region in 2002; some 260,000 in all. A direct income of €118m was generated for the city. On a per capita basis, Dublin earns twice as much in tourism revenue as Cork, and Galway four times as much. In 2005 €100,000 was given to the tourist board in 2005 for promoting the city (an increase of €73,600 from 2004) but a provision of €146, 000 was also made for 'twinning'.

So is there anything about Cork that is putting the tourists off? One reason might be an old prank played by locals on unsuspecting tourists, where the Cork fella would spot a tourist on St Patrick's Street, pull over and ask 'Excuse me, do you know the way to Montenotte?'

'I don't, sorry,' the tourist would say.

'Well, you go across St Patrick's Bridge, along McCurtain Street, up the hill to St Luke's, turn right and there you are.' Then he would drive off.

The old city of Cork was divided into quarters, formed by the line of the main street from north to south, and the mill stream running across; which is why the areas of the city were typically referred to using the points of the compass, as in the northwest district, etc. In medieval Cork the majority lived in lanes and alleys off the main street, plots of land known as burgage plots, measuring 20-25 feet wide and separated by fences with the plots extending right back to the city wall. The use of these strips of land was common in medieval town planning, particularly in English towns, where the fronts of houses were restricted spatially and back lanes were located at the end of the strips at the city walls for further access. With the exception of Main Street, Cork did not contain roads wide enough for even two carts to pass and the majority of lanes would not even permit two horses at a time.

For centuries Cork did not change. And it was not until 1787, when the city had expanded, that the corporation ruled that streets and houses should be properly numbered. Sixty-eight lanes led off the Main Street – 39 to the east and 29 to the west. These were inhabited by merchants and mayoral families. All but seven of the lanes were named after them. By the 1840s the city walls had disappeared, the watercourses were almost fully arched over and wider streets were coming in following the demolition of buildings, lanes and alleys. Only 22 lanes remained from the earlier number off Main Street, now named South and North Main Street.

Paul's Lane in Cork was formerly known as Codfill Lane. It led to the Coal Quay and was a badly lit area that also had a bad reputation. Crime and murder were so commonplace in this particular lane in eighteenth-century Cork, that the City Fathers found it necessary to erect gates at either end, which were closed at six o'clock and opened again at eight the following morning. They were taken down in the 1980s to build the shopping centre at St Paul's, but were put up again in 1985. The City Fathers' law has actually never been changed. Cork's Custom House was located nearby, in the building which is now the Crawford Art Gallery. Up to the end of the eighteenth century, ships could sail into the area, known as King's Quay. At the time, in the nearby King's Yard, contraband was burned, mostly tobacco, quite literally bringing tears to the eyes of Cork citizens.

Because of some of its bow-fronted, terraced buildings and winding main thoroughfare, Cork has been described as 'voluptuous'. Modern Catalan streetscape architect Beth Gali concurred but did not agree with the sentiment when she observed that St Patrick's Street did not hold a straight line and that it was instead full of bends. So she set about transforming it for the 2005 Capital City of Culture programme. Between 2002 and the summer of 2004 €13 million was required and to fund the project. The entire street was repaved with granite and limestone, traffic was confined to four lanes – two lanes 3.5 m wide each catering for general traffic, and two dedicated service lanes for buses and taxis, each lane at 2.5 m wide – and the pavements were widened to create plaza-like effects. The bane of the project for most Corkonians, however, were the tall lights that were supposed to resemble ships' masts, thereby reflecting the city's maritime culture. Perhaps Gali was unaware of Cork's flooding history when she said that she had 'tried to bring the spirit of the harbour into the city'.

The Cork City Development Plan – the result of two years of research by the City Planning Department – predicts a population increase in the Greater Cork area of 78,000 by 2020. This area encompasses the city and surrounding area extending out to Ballincollig, Blarney, Glanmire, Midleton, Cobh and Carrigaline. The bulk of the growth will be in what is referred to as 'Metropolitan Cork' – the part of the city which extends beyond the city boundary, but which is adjoining the city borough – where the plan predicts a growth of over 53,000. This will bring the population of the city over the 200,000 mark, with the Metropolitan area to over 280,000.

Let there be light

In 1708 the Corporation placed crude torches in Cork city by way of public lighting. The lamps burned rape oil, which was got from the yellow-flowered plants of the Rape Marsh at the lower end of the South Mall. Young boys then worked as 'link boys' waiting outside theatres and other places escorting people home with the torches. Girls at the time earned a few pennies acting as 'crossing sweepers' standing with a brush made from twigs and sweeping the path in front of the well-to-do.

In 1719, with the torches not proving to be much use, an act was passed which stated that it had been found by experience, that 'all cities well furnished with public lights in the dark nights are freer from murders, robberies, thefts, and other insolencies.' Cork was given a period of 21 years to provide lighting and by 1771, 200 'lamp irons' were installed at various locations around the city. On 9 May 1790, 1,600 lamps were counted; three years later another 34 were added. In 1822 the responsibility was vested in Cork's Wide Street Commissioners who contracted a London company to provide gaslights by 1825. By 1 January 1858, 1,100 gas lamps were lit in Cork but with prices so outrageous that a group of local businessmen founded the the Cork Consumers' Gas Company. They offered lower prices and were supported by the *Cork Examiner*. In 1936, electricity replaced gas for street lighting and the maintenance was assigned to the ESB (Electricity Supply Board).

One of the most important dates in the history of the city of Cork is 1690, the year of the Great Siege. William of Orange was not impressed with Cork for supporting the Catholic James II and sent the Duke of Marlborough to punish the citizens; he landed at Cork Harbour on 22 September 1690. He placed a canon on the tower of Red Abbey and fired on the walls of the city along the Grand Parade. He had an army of 1,000 and was supported by a Dutch army of 4,000. The Irish inside the city had an army of 5,000. Victory went to Marlborough. As bad as it was for the city, Cork could be thankful that Marlborough never turned his guns on the tower of the Red Abbey itself, which was and is the only structure that has survived from the medieval period. Another silver lining was that, with the walls severely damaged in the siege, little was done to repair them. By 1750 the walls were regarded as little more than a nuisance and were demolished in many places, which allowed the city to expand further; by the end of the eighteenth century almost none of the walls were left standing.

Water, water, everywhere, but what about the stink?

The city had begun to grow by the late seventeenth century, to the high ground of Shandon in the north and St Finbarr's in the south. Over the years the marshes, which lay to either side of the original city walls, were gradually reclaimed. The north-east marsh was first, which lay between St Patrick's Street and Lapp's Quay, followed by the east marsh area which takes in Oliver Plunkett Street. Dunscomb's Marsh, between St Patrick's Street and the South Mall, and Dunbar's Marsh (Morrison's Island) were all reclaimed from about 1680 and into the eighteenth century, as were Hammond's Marsh and Pike's Marsh, which lay to the west. The main thoroughfare (St Oliver Plunkett Street) became known as 'De Flat of De City'. Looking at Cork today, it is remarkable to think that in the sixth century there were a total of 365 islets in the Lee.

Cork, despite the reclamation, still continued to be a city of waterways, and when essayist Arthur Young visited it in 1776 while writing his *Tour of Ireland 1776-1779* (published in 1780) he wrote that Cork resembled 'a Dutch town, for there are many canals in the streets, with quays before the houses'. A lot of today's streets were formed when these waterways were covered over. But expansion did not necessarily make Cork a pretty picture. Docks and quays were unfenced and there was a high incidence of accidents with people falling into the river. Many slaughterhouses up in the Shandon area created filth which had only one place to flow – downwards into the city. After that, there was only one other place to put it – into the remaining marshes which eventually stank.

Lovers' Walk in Tivoli might not have been so popular with couples if they knew it had formerly been called Lepers' Road. The Lovers' Walk joins Montenotte, in the north-east part of Cork, called in Irish *Cnoc An Atinn*, the Hill of the Furze. Furze is the plant defined as having 'thorny shrubs with spine-shaped leaves' which should have made the place even less attractive to lovers. It is in the townland of Ballinabocht, the town of the poor, but the area had always been the residence of the wealthy Cork merchants. In the days of the Penal Laws (from 1691 until well into the nineteenth century) only Protestants could build houses there; a Papist was only allowed to build a cabin.

In 1804 a pig trap – a machine of sorts that was drawn by two horses – was introduced into the city. At the time, pigs were let roam around the streets to fatten on the rubbish but were eventually considered a nuisance. The machine worked but invariably led to another problem. When too many pigs were caught, they were kept inside by their owners, which meant that the streets became even filthier. Cork then became the 'dirtiest city in the empire'. According to the *Mercantile Chronicle* of 3 April 1805, it was also a dangerous city to walk around, with public drainage, rubbish and dodgy quays not just a contemporary complaint in Cork:

> Our total indifference, in this city, to everything which concerns our public accommodation and credit, has become a subject of wonder. Our nuisances seems to have a procreative power, and every day seems to shew some vexatious instance of their abominable fecundity. The day traveller … is often intercepted in his way by the lagoons of water, which the obstruction of the public sewers retain in the streets, and if he not be rode over by the gallopers … or run over by the cars … he may felicitate himself, on his return home, upon the cheap terms of such injury as he may receive in tumbling over a few of the many heaps of rubbish, which principally occupy our public ways. If the traveller by night escapes drowning … with the darkness of the lamps and the naked and unfenced state of the quays, to survive a night walk is become a matter of family thanksgiving.

Now that's Cork.

Cleanliness, at least efficient cleaning, was also forcibly kept at bay, as Morgan David discovered in 1819. David, who was not a member of the union, was employed as chimney sweep for a Mr Fitzgerald, who had invented a way for cleaning chimneys which dispensed with the need for using small boys ('climbing boys') to go up the inside of the chimney. (Possibly the invention was a type of joining brush that were used for years afterwards, but is referred to as a 'machine'.) The sweeps in Cork, who were an organised into a trade union, warned David not to use the machine for if it caught on, it would keep people out of a job. He ignored them and continued doing so until he was kidnapped and forced to 'renounce' the machine, which he did and the gadget was confiscated. Later he got a new one and began using it again. The sweeps broke into his house, attacked him and stole the machine. Four members of the 'Sooty Corporation' were later arrested and charged.

Arthur Young's comparing Cork to a Dutch city was not all that far off the mark. In 1719, Edward Webber, a Dutchman who was appointed town clerk of Cork after the Siege in 1690, in which many Dutchmen took part, offered to construct a raised embankment through the marshes from

Sheares Street (then Fenn's Quay) west to where the Lee divides into two channels. The public subscription was raised for what became known as the Mardyke Walk on 23 July 1766. It was named after the words *meer dyke*, which in Dutch means a sea dyke. The walk became an area much loved by the citizens, but at the beginning of the nineteenth century horses and cattle were also using it so in 1807 gates were erected at either end due to the pressure from pedestrian users. The walk reached its peak of popularity by the 1860s but more traffic and development meant the tranquillity suffered again, and by the 1920s the walk had lost its identity, with cyclists and business vehicles now gaining access. By the 1930s the quaint arched gas lamps, a feature of the walk, were replaced with electric ones. Real disaster struck in the 1940s when – ironically – Dutch Elm disease hit the trees and they had to be cut down. In 1952 the triple iron gates, nicknamed Hell, Heaven and Purgatory, were taken down. The name of the gentleman who had the keys to the gate was known locally as 'Rattling Dick'. Eventually, in 1977, a two-lane road was built and the 'walk' became more of a 'drive'. Cork's own anthem 'The Banks of my Own Lovely Lee' mentions the Mardyke, but for the sake of nostalgia, the trees are still included in the song.

How oft do my thoughts in their fancy take flight,
To the home of my childhood away
To the days when each patriot's vision seem bright
Ere I dreamed that these joys could decay.
When my heart was as light as the wild winds that
    blow
Down the Mardyke, through each elm tree
Where I sported and played, 'neath the green leafy
    shade
On the banks of my own lovely Lee.

Another line was written about the Mardyke, in the early-mid twentieth century. Not as poetic, but still striking in its brevity.

Does your mother ride a bike
On the Dyke
With a baby on the handlebars?

Now that's Cork for you.

Because Cork is built on marshy land, flooding is common in the city. On 1 November 1853 a devastating flood washed over the city, wiping out St Patrick's Bridge and North Gate Bridge. The *Illustrated London News*, however, were not so sympathetic in their reporting, describing the tragedy thus: 'The rains of Monday and Tuesday of that faithful week, as indicated by the gauge kept at the Royal Cork Institution of Mr. Humphrey's amounted to 2½ inches.' The quantity of rain for the two weeks before the flood was actually 11.9 inches, so Corkonians should really have suspected something. During the same period the previous year, only 3.87 inches were recorded. A more recent study in University College Cork (UCC) of the flood, calculated that, given the size of the Lee Basin – the source of the flood and an area of 562 square miles –2,000,000 cubic feet of water came rushing into Cork city that day. Thirt-one bridges in the county had to be replaced, including St Patrick's Bridge in Cork.

The most hilarious report of flooding, however, was back in January 1789, when a Cork newspaper described flooding of up to seven feet in depth on all the flat parts of the city. It began to subside about 9pm but the loss was considerable. The quays were swept away in many places, a ship broke away from its moorings and damaged St Patrick's Bridge which had just been built. 'But happily only one life was lost,' wrote the report, 'a man who was drowned and his name was Noah.' Now that's Cork.

Cork's first municipal housing scheme was completed in 1886 between Great William O'Brien Street and Watercourse Road in Blackpool. A total of 76 single-story houses were built on what had been the market site, at a cost of £85.10.0 each. They were badly needed. In one lane in Cork in the nineteenth century, Coleman's Lane, 423 people lived in 21 dwellings. By the 1940s only 27 people lived there in nine dwellings.

In the 1870s typhoid fever was a recurring nightmare in the city. The government, for some reason, could not figure out why and authorised an investigation. A Dr McCabe, an inspector for the Local Government Board, was appointed. The thinking was that the water was polluted. It had never occurred to them that a population of 78,000 people lived in 10,000 houses and only half had water closets and one-quarter had toilets. Most people took their water from wells. Things would eventually change, as testified by a proposal that was approved by the Director of Services on the following motion:

> That Cork City Council considers replacing the bathtubs in the bathrooms of Boyce's Street as the existing baths are approximately 2ft square and that the baths be replaced with showers for the disabled.

That was in February 2005. That same month, another proposal was referred to by the Council:

> That central heating would be installed as a matter of urgency in the remaining houses in Sunview, Fairhill that do not have central heating.

The Cork Pipe Water Company was founded in 1762 and water was pumped from about 80 feet above the city using a water wheel, to a reservoir, then down via a network of pipes. The pipes used at the time were wooden; each log being about 20 feet long and hollowed out. These timber pipes have turned up on various occasions during road works in Cork. Only low-lying parts of the city could get the water, and at a considerable charge of 2 guineas per annum from private householders and negotiated rates from other customers. The rest of the city's population and those who could not afford it used either the Lee or, later on, water pumps. However, an investigation of water pumps on 5 February 1843 revealed that only 7,141 visits were made to only five water pumps in the city and that there should be an increase in the number of pumps. It was argued that no house should be more than 200 yards from a water supply of sorts. It was also mooted that a prize should be given to the citizen with the cleanest home. How they cleaned the homes properly without water was not considered.

Pounding the pavements

The first attempt at paving the streets of Cork was in the 1730s, when black slabs were laid on the east side of the North/South Main Street in an area that became known as 'the flaggs' or 'de flaggs' (from Nos 13 to 52 Main Steet); an area of 600,530 square yards, or equal to about 124 acres. It made a bit of a fuss at the time because it was the only area that was paved. The Cork streets were introduced to the process of 'Macadamization' on 14 October 1827. But not everyone welcomed it. The *Southern Reporter* wrote:

> The close, damp and unhealthy weather is coming upon us, and we are preparing for it in such a way as to render it certain that we shall have as accompaniments, disease and contagion. The wise projectors who introduced the MACADAMIZATION of our streets, by strewing limestone as a substitute for pavement, may find the exposure of their ignorance in every place where the experiment has been tried ... The end of Patrick Street near the bridge – one of the widest avenues in the City – is an undulating mass of mud, in which any pedestrian who has the hardihood to attempt to cross from one side of the street to another runs some risk of being dangerously immersed.

In 1861 the Corporation began paving the streets with blocks. The first area was along Patrick's Quay. Some people who had observed the process in England commented on how inferior the process in Cork was, because deep ruts were being left between the blocks. Complaints were also made by a trader on Winthrop Street, when after three days the work had gone only as far as the third building and none of the gaps had been filled. There were only three workers involved on Winthrop Street, so the length of a building each was not bad going for Cork.

In 1912, the very Cork-sounding company, The Trinidad Lake Asphalt Paving Company, were contractors for a major road-surfacing programme. More recognisable possibly was the type of paving that was used – Durax Pavement. Durax blocks are sturdy durable blocks made from granite and have a worn appearance, not too dissimilar to cobblestone. As for the very Cork-sounding company, well, it actually has some Cork connections. Trinidad Lake Asphalt was a natural pitch from a lake in Trinidad, West Indies. The earliest mention of the deposit was in 1595 by Sir Walter Raleigh who used it as a sealant. Raleigh had lived in Cork for some time at Tivoli House, which is one of several places where he is said to have had his first smoke. In 1851 the asphalt was officially patented. They established a plant on Albert Quay to provide stone for the paving and the managing director of the company in Cork was a Corkman, Maurice Talbot Crosbie.

'One ticket to Farrandahadoremore, please.'
Cork's transport

As early as the 1820s, coaches belonging to the Cork and Dublin Commercial Union Car operated from Oliver Plunkett Street. A coach left every afternoon at 4pm and went via Fermoy, Cahir and Clonmel, stopped for 20 minutes at Carlow for breakfast and arrived in O'Connell Street at 1pm, making a total of 21 hours journey time.

Ireland was one of the pioneers of the railway age and the Act of Incorporation of the Great Southern and Western Railway on 6 August 1844 was to link Dublin and Cork by 165 miles of railroad, the longest inter-city line in Ireland and Britain at the time. Railways arrived in Cork in the 1840s from two directions. The Great Southern and Western Line reached Blackpool in 1849 and Penrose Quay in 1855. On the southside the Cork, Blackrock and Passage railway Terminus opened in 1850 on Victoria Quay (renamed Kennedy Quay after John F. Kennedy visited in 1963) and the Bandon Line on Albert Quay a year later.

The first tram appeared in Cork in 1872 – a horse-drawn tram connecting Cork, Blackrock and Passage railway stations with the Great Southern railway station at Glanmire Road. It went through St Patrick's Street in the city centre. The first electricity station in Cork was on Albert Road, and was called the Cork Electric Tramways and Lighting Company Ltd. The company catered for 35 trams across the city from December 1898 with the hub of the tram system being the Father Mathew Statue in St Patrick's Street. The trams operated from 7.30am to 11pm every day of the week. Cork finally bade farewell to its trams on 30 September 1931 with the arrival of bus services. Wilton (a suburb in the southwest) was once known as – wait for it – Farrandahadoremore, meaning the 'territory of the artist'. Can you imagine visitors trying to ask for the ticket? The name is no longer in use, but in the 1930s the buses that went to Wilton had the following on the front: 'Corsaire an Diolunaigh-Fearann an Dathadora'.

Taxis were always hard to come by in Cork, perhaps because it was in the new millennium – this millennium – before the Council figured out how to let the public know they were there. In January 2001, in response to the question of how to indicate the existence of a taxi rank, the following written reply was circulated at a meeting:

> The following signage/markings are required to indicate a taxi rank:
> a) An upright sign with the word 'taxi'.
> b) Roadway markings consisting of the word 'taxis'.

The number of taxis has increased in Cork since the liberalising of the taxi industry in 2000, with numbers in Cork rising from 216 to 719 in the first three years.

At the turn of the new millennium Cork seemed to be in pretty good shape with regard to its roads. There were 34km of national routes, 7km of regional routes, 349km of local roads, 121 traffic controlled junctions, 74 pedestrian signalised crossings, 16 zebra crossings, 1,400 public lighting lanterns, 6,000 controlled on-street car parking spaces and 1,350 off-street car parking spaces, 1 million m of regulatory road lines and 13,000 traffic, information and road signs. By 2003, there were 7,650 car parking spaces in the city centre of which 4,450 were off-street spaces in public car parks and 2,100 were on-street. The building of more multi-storey car parks in the city was then forbidden.

In August 2003 it was envisaged that the city would eventually grind to a standstill within twenty years if something was not done immediately. According to CASP (Cork Area Strategic Plan) the rise in car ownership and the projected population growth would have dramatic consequences if sustainable land use and transportation policies were not implemented. The forecast was that without intervention, traffic will double in the city in twenty years' time, peak-hour travel speeds will fall to five miles per hour on most roads in urban areas, and travel times to work will become up to five times longer than at present.

$\mathcal{A}$lthough Dublin is named as the most expensive city in the country, by 2004 Corkonians were paying over the odds for parking. Basement and ground-level parking spaces with apartments cost on average €20,000 in Limerick and Galway, and €45,000 in Dublin. A parking space with a new development in Cork city centre reached €80,000 in 2004, on top of the average €370,000 price of buying the home to go with it. The parking space was worth more than most cars that would use them. But spare a thought for the poor woman who, in May 2003, had to re-mortgage her home to pay a huge backlog of parking fines. The woman was facing more than 200 summonses for parking offences in Cork city until she strolled into City Hall and handed over a bank draft for €5,000. However, at that point, the parking fines section of Cork Corporation said that there were 23 fresh summonses before the court, which were not covered by the payment of the €5,000.

Clamping was introduced on 29 August 2001 and from then up to the end of May 2002, 3,810 vehicles were clamped and 3,190 vehicles were towed. The revenue from the clamping during that period was €96,000.

Cork, the city that sometimes sweeps
$\mathcal{H}$ow clean is Cork compared to other European cities? Let's look at the air first, since that is the

first thing tourists will take in when they arrive. Concentrations of contaminants in the air are measured in micrograms per cubic metre (ug/m3) with the belief that every 1ug/m3 reduction in particulates could increase average life expectancy by 1.5 to 3.5 days, about the length of time a visitor will spend in Cork. Annual average particulate levels across the UK are about 22 ug/m3. They are approximately 27 ug/m3 in London. The UK target is to reduce these to 20 ug/m3 in England and Wales, 18 ug/m3 in Scotland and 23-25 ug/m3 in London. Across Europe, average levels vary from 23 ug/m3 in Paris to 40 ug/m3 in Vienna. The average level in EU member states is 32 ug/m3. Cork comes in at 23-26 ug/m3 in the inner city, so that is, comparatively, not at all bad. However, in a Pfizer Healthy Neighbourhood Survey in October 2003, 75 per cent of Irish people were satisfied with the cleanliness of the air, streets and public places. The figure for Cork city was 69 per cent, just one below the German average of 70 per cent. The report was published in the *Examiner*, but not everyone celebrated the results. One man wrote in with his views. 'After having encountered eight dog droppings (one minute old) in a six-minute walk from my home to my workplace in Cork city I am left marvelling at this statistic and can assume it means one of three things:

(a) No Cork respondent to this survey has ever been in a German city

(b) Cork respondents have no problems with current levels of human and animal waste in the city or,

(c) Both of the above.

In fairness the man has a point. Encountering more than a poo a minute on a walk around Cork city would be very off-putting.

Corkonians became even more vexed when, at the end of 2004, it was announced that the annual bin charges would be increased to €255 (an added €175 on the previous year's charge). Finally, Cork got one up on Dublin, who pay only €80. The extra charge to Cork folk for living in the best city in the country is little consolation, particularly since there was the added €5 for each individual collection, which would make an average of €515 a year for emptying your bin in Cork. What would that actually get you if you lived there? The People's Republic of Cork, a sort of rebel watchdog group, compiled the following list:

If you were not charged the extra €75 'Cork tax' you could get:

(1) Almost 5,600 bags of Barry's Tea (based on 160 bag box)

(2) 48 pints of Murphy's

(3) Day trip to Amsterdam (Flights on 1st February direct from Cork with Aer Lingus €128 + €47 remaining for coffee shops and munchies).

(4) Buy a mooring space at Royal Cork Yacht Club in Crosshaven for a 55ft boat for a week and still have change for a few gin and ton-tons at the bar.

(5) Get a return bus to Dublin and get a helicopter lesson from Swiftair.

6) Buy a '1989 Toyota Carina for driving or parts €100' from buyandsell.ie. Spend the rest on wheel trims and furry dice.

That's Cork.

They should not really be complaining. Over a century or so ago, Corkonians paid a tax on windows. In the old city many windows were patterned and latticed to reduce the size of the panes of glass, doing likewise to the taxes on one's windows. The law stopped in 1876 but citizens are still clearly fearful of having too much glass in the house. In 2003 Cork was named as the top county in Ireland for the recycling of glass, recycling an average of 112 items of glass per household during the first eight months of 2004. With regard to waste in general, the council's plan is to reduce the quantity of municipal solid waste to be disposed of to landfill in the Cork region to 200,000 tonnes by the year 2020. The quantity of these wastes disposed of to landfill was 225,000 tonnes in 1995, and it is estimated that if the Waste Management Strategy is not implemented, this will have risen to 450,000 tonnes by 2020. Landfill had fallen from 137,000 tonnes in 2002 to just 93,000 tonnes in 2003. So they're on their way.

In the results in the 2003 Anti-Litter League, conducted by An Taisce (the National Trust for Ireland) Cork was placed in the 'litter black spot' category, the lowest of four categories. Things looked a bit better in 2004 when it moved into the 'moderately littered' category and – oh dear – in the year of its Capital of Culture tenure, it had moved into the 'serious litter problem' category. The corporation spends well over €3 million annually on street cleaning, which includes a €30,000 budget for cleaning up chewing gum.

In 1999, the cleaning up of the River Lee became a priority with the entire raw sewage output of the city dumped untreated into the river. This included 13 million gallons of wastewater as well as 20 tonnes of solid matter (an ill-defined term, but the imagination can make up for the lack of definition). Cork City Council had been tinkering with the idea for many years and in the 1960s and 1970s about £20 million was spent laying new sewers along the north and south quays to catch and collect waste water. The cost of the drainage works in 1999 was estimated at £100 million, with a time period of three years. But by the end of 2004 the scheme was still unfinished and it was getting closer to the €300 million mark (at €254 million). It was beneficial for the city in one sense because with all the digging going on people could get a decent view of what it was like in the good old days of canals and waterfronts before they were covered over. Confidence in the project had risen when the first Lee Swim, a race that went back to the 1930s and was last held in 1987, returned in 2005.

Cork's buildings:
the good the bad and the ugly

You've got to hand it to them – Cork's great clocks
Cork's most famous church, St Anne's Church in Shandon, was built in 1722 to replace the older church of St Mary's which was destroyed in the siege of 1690. Rumour has it that it was built in sandstone for the south and west, and the north and east in limestone, because two contractors, one owning a sandstone quarry, the other limestone, agreed to share the contract. The tower, which stands 170 ft high, was added in 1749 and is legendary for the clock with its four faces. The clock was the idea of – brace yourself for the name – Councillor Delay, in 1843, who complained of the hardship suffered by the city's working class, most of whom had no watches and could not tell the time. He was supported by members of the medical profession who agreed that people were at risk of poisoning themselves if they were not taking medication at the

right time as a result of having no watches or clocks in their homes. An inscription on one of the clocks reads:

passenger, measure your time, for time is the measure of being.

However, the clock is known as 'the four-faced liar' because high winds from different directions have given each of the hands on each clock a different time – the minute hands on the east and west faces gain on their neighbours on the north and south faces. Whether or not people have died taking medication at the wrong times as a result is not recorded. But there is a Cork joke about an American who asked why the clock showed different times. He was told that if they all told the one time they would need only one clock. A perfectly valid reason indeed.

Cork architect and clockmaker James Mangan got the commission for the Shandon Steeple clock and it was installed in 1847 at the height of the Famine. The four-metre long weather vane at the top of the steeple is in the shape of a fish, known in Cork as 'the goldy fish', and was chosen to reflect the salmon industry in Cork at the time. The details of the clock, which is one of the largest in Europe, are as follows:

Four dials, over fifteen feet in diameter. Four sets of hands with a weight of over five cwt (hundred weight, one cwt is the equivalent to 112 lbs, or eight stone). The frame of the clock is fourteen feet by four feet wide and five feet high, and with the machinery weighs more than two and a half tons. The striking hammer weighs 100 pounds and falls through a space of twelve inches. The chime hammers, four of them, each weigh 26 pounds. The pendulum is fourteen feet long and the ball weighs three cwts.

Mangans's Jewellers (of the Shandon fame) opened in 1817 on St Patrick's Street and outside the shop was erected a large pedestal clock which served as a good focal point on the street. The mechanism for the clock – which appears to be freestanding – was powered by a shaft running through a basement under the street. The shaft was driven by a large weight which hung from the second floor of the shop. In 1920 a British auxiliary lobbed a grenade into the shop blowing out all the windows, but the store survived. Nothing could save it from the swinging balls of Cork, however, and in the 1980s it was demolished to make way for the Merchant's Quay Shopping Centre. The town council insisted that the famous clock stayed put.

In 1876 an agreement was made between the postmaster general in London and the Cork

Harbour Commissioners for a system of electric time signals from Greenwich to the Cork telegraph office. If visitors were confused by the Shandon clock, then they were certainly disorientated by the time signal. A large gun, a relic from the Crimean War, was fired each day at 25 minutes to one, which was Greenwich noontime (Cork is 5° west of Greenwich). All the clocks in the city would be set from this gun. The gun went out of action in the 1920s.

George, Goldy, the trumpet and the dismembered elk
In 1734 the medieval church of St Finbarre had to be demolished because of its bad repair. William Burgess won a competition for a new design in 1862 and the new cathedral was built between 1865 and 1876, the spires of which are now perhaps Cork's greatest landmark. Disappointed competitors (who described the building as an 'unsightly edifice') gave him a hard time over certain aspects of his design, but the main objection was that the competition only provided for £15,000 and the design would cost £30,000. In answering the objection, Burgess, in a reply in the *Cork Constitution*, said that no cathedral worthy of its name could be built for £15,000 and that everything essential for divine service would be provided for. In total the cathedral cost £100,000. When the cathedral was finished, Burgess made a gift to the

city: a golden gilded six-foot statue of an angel with a trumpet in either hand standing 100 feet from the ground and known to Corkonians as the 'goldy angel'. Cork myth has it that when the trumpets sound, the world will come to an end. But in December 1998, someone was paranoid enough to steal the trumpets, possibly hoping to evade the inevitable. At the time, the cathedral was being renovated and although there was scaffolding around the building, it fell well short of the goldy angel. The trumpets were also nailed into the statue by four-inch nails, so whoever had stolen them was certainly driven by a serious sense of purpose. Thankfully, within 48 hours, the trumpets were found in waste ground close to St Patrick's Catholic Church, on the other side of the city, and replaced. Why they were stolen and who stole them remains a mystery. But that's Cork.

Another St Finbarr's, Finbarr's South on Dunbar Street, is the earliest Catholic Church in Cork, dating to 1766. The altar contains the much-praised figure the 'Dead Christ' by one of Ireland's most famous sculptors, John Hogan (1800-58). Hogan was born in Waterford but came to Cork to work for the Deanes, Cork's famous architects. Only two other copies of the 'Dead Christ' exist. One in the Carmelite Church in Dominick Street, Dublin, which is supposed to have been crafted by Hogan's son. The third is in the Basilica of St John the Baptist in faraway St John's, Newfoundland. The statue itself, although famous, was actually modelled on an ordinary man, the rabble-rousing son of a Cork merchant named Duncan, who as punishment for his unruliness, had to grow his hair for months to model for the work.

The hills of Cork have been well utilised; Shandon's steeple and the triple spires of St Finbarre's appear at the focal point of many views of the city. The statue of Fr Mathew on St Patrick's Street however is really the hub for Cork people. The bronze statue was designed by sculptor John Henry Foley and unveiled by John Maguire, founder of the *Examiner* on 10 October 1864. Later, the trams would radiate from this point, as would the buses, which replaced the trams in 1931. Fr Mathew was the man responsible for the Temperance movement, with the slogan 'Ireland sober, Ireland free'. On 10 April 1838 only 39 people signed up, but eventually the numbers swelled. He died on 8 December 1856 and was buried in Cork's St Joseph's Cemetery, formerly the Botanic Gardens, which he purchased in 1830 as a burial place for the poor, since no such graveyard existed at the time. His funeral procession numbered 50,000. The population of Cork was then 64,000.

In 1760 Cork Corporation decided to erect a statue to honour George II, who had died of a stroke that October. A Dutchman named Van Nost was commissioned as the sculptor and on 7 July 1761 the statue was unveiled. It was placed in the centre of Tuckey's Bridge – which connected Tuckey's Quay (now part of the Grand Parade), and George's Street, which was later changed to the present Oliver Plunkett Street – with the following words:

> The citizens of cork erected this statue to the memory of King George the Second in gratitude for the many blessings they enjoyed in his auspicious reign MDCCLXII.

The statue was quickly called 'George a-horseback' and when it was moved to the southern end of Grand Parade and painted a golden-yellow colour the statue became known as the Yellow Horse or the Yalla Horse, or, in Irish, *An Capall Buí*. This is the origin of the Irish name of the street, which is *Sráid an Chapaill Bhuí*, the street of the Yellow Horse. Not all citizens agreed they were blessed during George's reign, and the statue was a constant target for vandals and pranksters. On 4 June 1795 it was recorded that 'persons attempted to mutilate the statue of George II on Grand Parade' and a reward of £400 was offered to catch

the offenders. Then on 11 May 1803 it was recorded
that 'several articles of wearing apparel, which were
indecently hung upon the railing round the statue on
the Grand Parade, were seized by the sheriffs'. As
the British monarchs changed, the heads of the statue changed, and eventually the statue began to lean
badly to one side and had to be supported by wood-
en crutches under the horse and the right arm of
George II. On 3 March 1862 the figure of George
mysteriously fell from his perch. Whoever it was that
knocked down George's statue remains unknown,
despite the offer of a reward. Cork Corporation
removed the entire structure and created a green
space where the statue had stood. Local tradition
claims that the last person known to have possession of the head of poor George II was a Mr Morton,
a gunsmith in Cork in the late nineteenth century. A
local rhyme was penned for posterity:

> Into the Lee there's a heavy splash
> And the King who once sat stiff as starch
> Was nowhere on the fourth of March
> Eighteen hundred and sixty-two.

Another statue that caught more than the public's attention was the life-size bronze statue of the
great Irish elk, an animal that became extinct 5,000
years ago. Following an open competition run by
Cork County Council in 1994, the fourteen foot high

bronze elk, with antlers spanning twelve feet, was placed in a prime position overlooking the new Cork-Mallow highway. The sculptor, Kevin Holland, used bronze that was reinforced to guard against vandals, employing bronze sheets overlapping a stainless steel frame, and the statue was an exact replica of the original species. The council commissioned the work as part of the EU campaign to adorn motorways with interesting works of art. However, in May 1996, Holland noticed that something was missing after his attention was drawn to scratch marks on the scrotum of the statue. A closer inspection revealed that elk's penis had been robbed. A shocked Holland figured that whoever had removed the elk's penis knew something about metalwork as well as basic anatomy, but had no idea why anyone would want to steal it. The statue had cost £20,000.

Adieu! Ye roaring captives in the North Gate!

There were two main prisons in Cork before the city began to expand in the eighteenth century: Southgate Prison and Northgate Prison, built at both bridges. The Northgate Prison was in a ruinous state and it was replaced in 1715 with solid, hewn stone and facings of white limestone. All well and good, but it was no use as a prison because it had no gallows and no place to spike heads. So it was used as a debtor's prison only. Debtor prisoners at the time were not allowed rations, so they hung hats or receptacles from cords through the bars and down onto the streets to beg.

The west of Cork city in the nineteenth century contained the larger public institutions – the city and county gaols on opposite banks of the Lee and the lunatic asylum, the largest in Ireland in 1847.

If you ever believed that Cork was a city of contrasts, compared to the slums, prisons and madhouses on the west side, the east side was inhabited by the professionals and in 1845, thirteen of 98 lawyers had separate work and home addresses; in 1863 this number had increased to half. A visitor to Cork during this period, a Scotsman, Robert Graham, dropped into the County Gaol and noted that only twenty of the 309 inmates were protestants – sixteen of them debtors. He also noted the drop over the main gate, which from 'motives of humanity' was made not from hemp but from silk.

Ireland in Pictures, a book of 400 photographs and comments, was published by a Chicago publisher in the 1890s (J.S. Hyland). Clearly sympathetic with the Cork people, accompanying the picture of Cork's asylum, the commentary read:

> To minister to a mind diseased is, indeed, a noble charity, and, unfortunately, in Ireland there is a great

need of it ... Some English writers, oddly enough, have attempted to account for it on the ground that the Irish people, who formerly drank milk almost exclusively at their meals, have become confirmed tea-drinkers ... The Irish themselves laugh heartily at this English theory, and say it is not tea, but British rule, that is making them mad.

The church of SS Peter and Paul, which sits hidden a few yards back from St Patrick's Street, was designed by Edward Welby Pugin (1834-75) after what was described as a 'memorable competition' in 1859; memorable in that the selection committee were said to be composed of retailers of soap, tea and whiskey instead of architects. The winner was Pugin, the son of architect A.W.N. Pugin, who had died insane at the age of 40 while working on the Palace of Westminster. Much of his energy was spent in very costly and very pointless litigation to prove that his father's contribution to the Houses of Parliament was greater than that of Charles Barry, whom he worked with on the buildings. Like his father, Edward also ended his days in a lunatic asylum.

Queens College Cork was founded in 1845 and became part of the NUI (National University of Ireland) in 1908. Other universities incorporated in Belfast, Cork and Galway were known as the

Queens Universities by the establishment, and as 'Godless colleges' by the Catholic hierarchy, since Jews, Catholics (and any Protestant dissenters) were all barred. Education for these groups was given by charity schools, such as the Christian Brothers, who set up their first school in Cork in 1820. Eight months after the college building in Cork was completed, the registrar wrote to the board of works complaining that the bursar's office was still without a door. Of all the rooms that needed a door it surely would have been the one that held the money. Other defects were more pressing. Adjacent to the university gates was one of the city gaols and it was deemed inappropriate for staff and students to enter the college through a prison gate. Another entrance was built and the gaol entrance, a fine Doric portico, was then incorporated into the future development of UCC.

The buildings of Cork – out with the new, in with the old
$\mathcal{A}$ point of interest regarding Cork's buildings is that brick was never a traditional medium for construction as there were few local kilns. However, (back to the Dutch connection) Dutch bricks were not uncommon in many eighteenth-century buildings. These came into the city because Cork traded with Holland a lot and ships returned to Cork using bricks as ballast. The houses near the Imperial Hotel on the

South Mall were made from yellow Dutch brick.

Cork has no formal squares like those of Georgian Dublin. It has some fine examples of Georgian buildings, however, such as those on the North Mall and the Imperial Hotel on the South Mall. The Victoria Hotel appears in James Joyce's *A Portrait of the Artist as a Young Man*, where he had 'drisheen' for breakfast before heading to the Mardyke and the college, but it was in the Georgian building, the Imperial Hotel, that he stayed at the age of twelve when he came to Cork with his father to sell the last of the family's properties. The great Irish painter, Daniel Maclise also stayed in the Imperial Hotel. William Thackery met Fr Theobald Mathew in the hotel also. For tea. Charles Dickens gave a reading there while he was in Cork and finally it was there that Liszt gave a piano recital.

There were five Martello Towers in use in Cork Harbour, although the name has little to do with Cork. In 1794 the British frigates *HMS Juno* and *HMS Fortitude* were beaten off the island of Corsica, which they were trying to capture, by strong gunfire at a place called Mortella Point. They came back and took the tower but the design was so impressive they decided to use it in case of an attack by Napoleon. Mortella means 'myrtle' and refers to the trees that were abundant in Corsica, but the name was misspelt, either by accident or design, by the British. The five towers in Cork, built from 1815, are at Haulbowline, Rosslague, Belvelly, Monning (Fota) and Ringaskiddy. Monning is the only Irish tower ever to be attacked and that was on St Stephen's Day 1867 by the Fenians. Nobody was hurt. Napoleon did intend to invade Britain, possibly by balloon.

At a cost of exactly £613,315.6 when it opened in 1968, Cork's County Hall is Ireland's tallest building and not, as is commonly believed, Liberty Hall in Dublin. County Hall is 212 feet high while Liberty Hall is 195 feet high. The reason Corkonians do not brag about it as much is that it is even uglier than Liberty Hall (but not as ugly as Cork's bus station, criticised for over 30 years as one Ireland's greatest urban eyesores). Cork Corporation received a planning application for a major refurbishment of the building and the erection alongside it of a new, six-storey edifice. The estimated cost of the proposals is about £30 million. Designed by Patrick McSweeney, then Cork County architect, County Hall is the only post-1940 building in the city listed for protection and in its appeal to An Bord Pleanala (planning department), An Taisce said the building formed 'a striking monumental landmark' on the westerly approaches to Cork.

They have a bad habit of taking over listed buildings, but the citizens of Cork should really have stopped the fast food outlets moving into the former store of Woodford Bourne grocers and wine merchants at the end of St Patrick's Street. The company is the descendant of a firm of wine merchants named Maziere and Sainthill, established in Cork around 1750. In the mid-nineteenth century the widow of grocer John Woodford married a Mr Bourne and together bought the stock of the wine merchant, Sainthill. The shop was taken over by an Englishman, James Adam Nicholson, and was known as one of the best-stocked shops in Cork. In 1980, Mandy's fast food took over the premises and in the mid-1980s McDonalds moved in. Apart from the Virgin Megastore across the way, once the site of the Queen's Old Castle, it is a serious blemish on the cityscape of Cork. We could mention a few around the Coal Quay area also, but let's leave it at that.

The Cork City Centre Better Buildings Awards in 2003 highlighted a glaringly obvious flaw in the city, in that the first prize in every category went to old buildings. The categories ranged from best retail frontage to best pub, but no modern buildings scooped the first prize. The best retail frontage went to Lynes and Lynes, an antique shop in Victorian red brick on MacCurtain Street; the best pub front is at the Bodega, a nineteenth century limestone front on Cornmarket Street; the best commercial frontage is at O'Flynn Exhams, a firm of solicitors on South Mall which occupies a restored Georgian red brick building; the best signage was at The Mardyke, a converted limestone warehouse on Sheares Street; and finally the best 'new' development was CDGA Engineering in a restored Victorian red-brick location on Patrick's Quay. In 2004, the Retail Shop Front winner went to Veritas on Carey's Lane; the best pub front to Bodega, again; the best commercial business frontage to the Anglo Irish Bank, Anglesea Street; the best new development to Anglo-Irish Bank, Anglesea Street, a bit stuck there on that last one. And finally, the best signage to – stuck again – The Mardyke, Sheares Street.

Cork as a capital of culture

Voices from the gods: Cork, culture and the Opera House

In 1825 there were eleven flint glass factories and three houses in Cork: the Cork Glass Company, the first one established in 1783; The Waterloo Glass Company; and the Terrace Glass Company. Over 150 glass blowers and glasscutters produced some of the finest crafts in Britain at the time. By 1850 the industry was as good as extinct. The Cork Glass Company had closed in 1818; the Waterloo Glass Company in 1835; and the Terrace Glass Company in 1841. The reasons for the demise of the industry seem to be a source of conjecture, but one reason cited was that a lot of glass was blown in Birmingham and taken to Cork for cutting because of the high reputation it had, then re-exported. There was a strike in Cork and the masters and men could not agree. It continued for over two years and the men were being paid from Birmingham. At the end of two years the factory owners were ruined and when the strike money was discontinued from Birmingham, so were the men. Silver was also a thriving industry in Cork, and just for the record, the famous moving statue of Ballinspittle was made in Cork city, at Bernard's Statue Shop in the French Quarter (where the Paul Street Shopping Centre now stands) by Maurice O'Donnell in 1954.

"The Great Exhibition of the Works of Industry of all Nations' was held in the Crystal Palace in Hyde Park, London, from 1 May to 15 October 1851. At the exhibition were many of Cork's leading citizens including John Francis Maguire, founder of the *Cork Examiner* and architect Sir Thomas Deane. Belfast, Dublin, even Limerick were well represented but there was little from Cork. With hurt pride, the concept of a Cork exhibition was mooted and eventually what began as a provincial display became a national one. The success of the Cork Exhibition on 10 September 1852 in turn hurt the pride of the Dubliners who had their own the following year in 1853, even poaching the architect, Sir John Benson, who was responsible for adapting the Corn Exchange Building (which stood near the present City Hall). Cork had a lot to show off apart from arts and crafts, with the following also said to be amply represented:

Whiskey, ale, porter, pearl barley, Norton's Projectile Shells ... stuffed birds, wax flowers and Cork

Ginghams.' The majority of Cork businesses and manufacturers also took part, even individuals including 'Mr. Abraham Hargrave, of Ballynoe, an 'amateur mechanic', [who] exhibited his improved batteries.

When the National Exhibition ended in Cork, the buildings stood empty. A site was chosen between the Old Custom House and the north channel of the Lee (where the present Opera House now stands) for an 'Athenaeum', a centre for the arts in Cork. So the structure that served as the Fine Arts Hall in the exhibition was dismantled and taken across the river for this purpose in 1855. Not wholly adequate for performances, mostly because of poor acoustics, it reopened – altered and enlarged – in 1877 as the Theatre Royal and Opera House. The first performance that night was a play by British dramatist, Henry James Byron, *Our Boys*. The last show was the romantic comedy, *The Belle of New York*, before an electrical fault caused the fire which destroyed the Opera House on 12 December 1955. Cork had no major theatre for a decade until the opening of the Michael Scott-designed new Opera House on the same site. It was opened by President de Valera on 31 October 1965.

Architect Michael Scott, who designed what many people believe is one of Dublin's greatest eyesores, the Abbey Theatre, used the Opera House at Malmo, Sweden, as a reference for his Opera House in Cork. Because the building in Malmo is located in a parkland area, the first location proposed for the Opera House was beside the river on the Western Road, where Jurys Hotel stands now. The thinking was that it would add to the skyscape already dominated by the spires of St Finbarre's Cathedral and would be bordered a couple of hundred yards away by the entrance gates of UCC. With the south channel of the Lee flowing past it, all the elements were there for the perfect setting. However, despite being only a ten-minute stroll (and good enough for Jurys) from the centre of Cork, the location was not considered central enough. The idea of using brick in the construction of the building – which would have sat well with the Crawford building next to it – was another idea that was shelved because of the expense. Instead, Cork got the aluminium, concrete and glass edifice that dismayed citizens until yet another revamping in 1995, which included windows in the north-facing wall – always considered an eyesore – and an electronic advertising screen.

Tickets for the 'gods' area of the Opera House could not be pre-booked in the early 1900s, and these seats, sold earlier, were known as the 'early door' tickets. This meant that people had to queue on the steps that were running up the side of the Opera House until the doors were opened. Queuing could begin as early as six o'clock, when there would be a mad rush for the doors as tickets were sold on a first come first served basis. The people who sat in the gods were generally the real Corkonians who liked to be as active as possible during performances. Some great heckling stories have been handed down from the gods. Well, from the area known as the gods.

During what was supposed to have been a very dull performance of *The Diary of Anne Frank*, the point was reached where the Nazis broke into the house where she was in hiding. One audience member, having seen enough, shouted 'She's under the stairs!'

At a religious revival meeting at the Opera House a woman from Northern Ireland was on stage telling of her religious experiences.

'Last night I was in the arms of Satan,' she said, 'but tonight I am in the arms of Jesus.'

'How are you fixed for tomorrow night?' shouted one of the audience.

When a British Drama Group were doing a week-long stint at the Opera House the play was said to be dreadful. The whole first act was set in a remote country cottage and consisted only of a wife and husband engaged in lengthy dialogue. At the beginning of the second act there was a knock on the door.

'I wonder who that could be?' asked the wife.

'For God's sake just let them in,' shouted someone from the gods.

Finally, during one performance of a play an actress had to jump into a river that had been painted on the stage beside a papier maché rock. Upon jumping, her line was:

'River of my race receive me'. Jump she did, and landed hard with a thud on the boards.

'Oh my goodness,' came the response from one of the audience, ''tis frozen.'

Communicating All True Intelligence – Cork in words and print

The famous Cork song 'The Bells of Shandon' was written by Father Prout, whose real name was Francis O'Mahoney, a Jesuit priest from Blarney, whose family owned the Blarney Woollen Mills. He was born in Cork in 1804 and died in Paris in 1866. He became well known in the literary set in London and wrote for *Fraser's Magazine*, the forerunner of *Punch*, using the pseudonym of Father Prout. Another legendary Cork folk song, 'The Boys of Fair Hill' was written by Sean

Callaghan, Fair Hill being in the north side of the city, where there has always been competition with the south side. This is one of the best-known Cork songs and 'De Boys' – as it has become known – was sung regularly at public gatherings. Originally it was a song in praise of the traditional pastimes – bowling, drag-hunting and hurling – and a few of the north city landmarks were mentioned, such as Quinlan's Pub in Blackpool. But eventually the lyrics were corrupted and many versions now exist. The song also inspired poetic lines such as 'The Blackpool girls are very small up against the sunbeam wall. The Montenotte girls are very rude; they go swimming in the nude.' Callaghan also wrote odd and eccentric songs, as in the poem called 'Connie Doyle's Armoured Car' which was actually about a dog named Ringwood, famous for winning drag hunts, a sport that involved laying a scent and letting loose competing hounds on a trail of roughly ten miles. The first dog home – and presumably this dog was regularly home first if he became the subject of a song – was the winner. Judging by the lyrics, this was no ordinary dog and was actually referred to as 'the armoured car', an odd title for a canine.

> He had cast-iron jaws and steel-padded paws
> Every nail was like an iron bar
> From one mile to ten he would never give in
> If you ran him from here to Castlebar.

Apparently it was written ad lib in a pub, which would explain the dodgy use of Castlebar to get the final rhyme. (Castlebar is also 139 miles from Cork, not one or ten. But we'll let him away with it.)

$\mathcal{B}$efore the *Cork Examine*r (the *Irish Examiner* since 1996) appeared on 30 August 1841, the *Cork Constitution*, a largely Unionist paper, was the main newspaper in Cork. John Francis Maguire was the founder of the *Examiner*, initially an evening paper coming out only three days a week, becoming a six-day morning paper in the hands of Thomas Crosbie in 1858. Crosbie introduced the *Evening Echo* in 1892, a paper that has become a great part of Cork life and lore. Known as '*de paper*', de sellers became known as de Echo Boys and many were known by dere nicknames – Whacker, Doc, Con Con, Robot and Wallo. De origins of de names can be left up to de imagination.

$\mathcal{T}$he first paper to be printed in Ireland was actually printed in Cork by Oliver Cromwell, who, after terrorising the country, came to Cork to put his feet up for the winter. Figuring he had done a good job round the country, he printed a newspaper to record the events of his campaign. The paper was called the *Irish Monthly Mercury*, mercury being a common name for papers in England. It praised Cromwell and bemoaned the fact that he was going back to England. It was published on 21 December 1649. Another paper published in 1650 (until some time in the 1680s) in Ireland was called the *Irish Mercury Monethly Communicating All True Intelligence*. Must have been published in Cork as well, so.

In the course of the eighteenth century there were five papers in Cork – all published in the English language: *The Cork News Letter*, *The Medley*, *The Cork Evening Post*, *The Hibernian Chronicle* and *The Cork Journal*. The number of Irish-speaking people in the city was 10,381 in 1851, dropping to 7,201 in 1891. The total population was 85,732. However, one half of the circulation of the *Journal of the Gaelic League* (Connradh na Gaeilge) was in Cork city and county by 1894. The Gaelic League was founded by Douglas Hyde in 1893 to promote the use of Irish. Hyde became made the first president of Ireland in 1938.

Poet Edmund Spenser was married in Cork and had an estate in north Cork. Although he made Ireland his home he supposedly despised the Irish and was of the opinion that the only solution was to exterminate the natives altogether. In 1580, was appointed secretary to the Lord Deputy of Ireland in 1580, Lord Grey, and he himself was named Sheriff of the County of Cork in 1598. In October of that year an insurrection broke out in Munster. The rebels set fire to Kilcolman Castle, Spenser's residence near Doneraile, and although he and his wife escaped, their child died in the flames. He was a broken man and died three months later in London. It was at this residence that Spenser wrote most of 'The Faerie Queen' and not in Cork city as some believe. The river mentioned in the poem is the river that ran through the estate:

Sat among the coolie shade
Of the greene alders by the Mullae's shore.

In 1916, Daniel Corkery (1878-1964) teacher, Gaelic League activist and leading literary figure in Cork in that era, publishing *Threshold of Quiet* in 1916 and *Hidden Ireland* in 1927, described Cork as follows:

Leaving us the summer visitor says in good-humoured way that Cork is quite a busy place, considering how small it is. And he really thinks so, because whatever little we have of pastors, postmen, urchins, beggars; of squares, streets, lanes, markets; of wagons, motors, tramcars, ships; of spires, turrets, domes, towers; of bells, horns, meetings, cries; concert halls, theatres, shops – whatever little we have all these – as humdrum a collection of odds-and-ends as ever went by the name of city – are flung higgledypiggedly together into a narrow, double-streamed, many-bridged river valley, jostled and jostling, so compacted that the mass throws up a froth and flurry that confuses the stray visitor, unless indeed he is set on getting at the true size and worth of things. For him this is Cork. But for us it is only 'the flat of the city'.

Corkery in his teachings – he taught at the Christian Brothers National School, founded the Cork Dramatic Society and in 1931 became Professor of English at UCC – greatly influenced two of Cork's greatest modern literary figures, Seán O'Faoláin (born 1900) and Frank O'Connor (born 1903), novelists and short-story writers who had a great influence on Irish fiction.

Seán O'Faoláin was born John Francis Whelan in Cork city on 22 February 1900 and was educated at UCC. He went to Harvard in 1926, completing a Masters on Yeats. He married Eileen Gould, a fellow Corkonian, in Boston in 1928. After working as a teacher in London, he returned to Ireland in 1933 with an advance from publishers Jonathan Cape for writing *Midsummer Madness and Other Stories*. His first novel, *A Nest of Simple Folk,* followed and in 1940 he founded the Dublin literary magazine, *The Bell*, a magazine that mostly published fiction, including contributions from writers Flann O'Brien, Elizabeth Bowen and Frank O'Connor. O'Faolain wrote a lot for *Playboy* magazine between 1966 and 1974 and his collected stories appeared in the 1980s. He died in Dun Laoghaire, Dublin, on 20 April 1991.

Yeats said that Frank O'Connor did for Irish literature what Chekhov did for Russian literature. Born Michael O'Donovan in Cork city in 1903, he took his mother's maiden name, O'Connor, later, as a writer. He was an only child, and devotes a good deal of his autobiography to his mother. He left school at fourteen and served in the IRA during the Civil War. However, his disappointment over Irish Republicanism was reflected in his first collection of stories, *Guests of the Nation* (1931). He became a director of the Abbey Theatre in 1935 but resigned in 1939, going to America and writing regularly for the *New Yorker*, who published 45 of his stories. When he returned to Ireland in 1941, censorship prevented him from being published, a ban that was lifted in 1945. He had married a Welsh actress, Evelyn Bowen, in 1939, a marriage that ended in 1949. He left for America again in 1952 and married once more in 1953, this time to American Harriet Rich. He died in Dublin on 10 March 1966.

Glory be to Jeyes' fluid – theatre, cinema and fleapits in Cork

Trying to locate the first actual theatre in Cork is a difficult task since there was no shortage of buildings where performances were put on but were not actually considered theatres. The earliest theatre was probably at Dingle Lane, off Kyle Street, and was converted from a house in 1713 by the Dublin Smock Alley Theatre Company and closed in 1742. In 1759 Spranger Barry came to Cork from the Crow Street Theatre Company in Dublin. And on 21 July 1760 he opened the Theatre Royal at the present post office on Oliver Plunkett Street. The first play that evening was *The Orphan*. The theatre was modelled on the Crow Street Theatre in Dublin and had the same dimensions – 136 feet long by 60 feet wide. The building and all the contents were destroyed by fire on 1 April 1840. Cork's second theatre was built in 1853 and kept the old name of The Theatre Royal. During the mid 1860s it was able to seat 2,000 patrons. Remodelled from the designs under the direction of Sir John Benson, the refurbished and enlarged Theatre Royal reopened on 26 December 1867 and flourished until 1875 when it was sold to the postal authority. After much alteration it opened two years later as Cork's General Post Office.

The first moving picture shown in Cork was on 29 April 1896 at a fair in aid of the Munster Convalescent Home. It was held in the Assembly Rooms on South Mall. The show was simply called

Splendid Living Pictures and it took place just over a week after the first ever screenings in Ireland when the Star of Erin Theatre in Dublin showed The Cinématographe. Dubliners, however, were supposed to have been unmoved by the Cinématographe, which showed an acrobat fighting a cat, and a Scottish drummer.

James Joyce opened the Volta cinema in Dublin on 20 December 1909 with plans to do likewise in Cork. However, only a week after the Dublin cinema opened, The Electric Theatre began operating on Maylor Street, off St Patrick's Street in Cork, and was billed as 'The Newest and Cheapest Entertainment in the South of Ireland'. It was the first official cinema in the city and the opening day saw *Three Great Thrills* screened, including *A Dash for the North Pole* and *The Derby of 1909* (the whole thing was screened from start to finish). The cinema went out of business at the end of January 1910.

Despite the curfew during the War of Independence, the Pavilion cinema opened on 10 March 1921 on St Patrick's Street, with the film *The Greatest Question* by D.W. Griffith, who also directed *The Birth of a Nation*. The cinema and its restaurant were one of the most cosmopolitan venues in the city for over 60 years until August 1989 when it closed its doors. The last film to be shown was fittingly, *Indiana Jones and the Last Crusade*.

It is debatable whether or not the first official sound film to be shown in Cork was *The Leatherneck*, screened in the Opera House on 11 June 1929. The film was nominated for an Oscar in 1930 under the Best Writing category and was actually classed as 'silent' or 'part-talking'. The Pavilion was the first cinema to have a full sound system, installed in August 1929, which inspired other Cork cinemas to do likewise very quickly and competition became fierce.

The Palace on McCurtain Street, which would eventually become the Everyman Theatre, advertised itself as 'The House with the Perfect Sound' when the 'talkies' proper arrived in the 1930s. However, its greatest success ironically was *City Lights*, a silent film that was shown in November 1931 and starred Charlie Chaplin, whose mother, Hannah Hill, was a Cork native. The Lido cinema in Blackrock retorted by billing itself as 'The House with the *More* Perfect Sound'. The Palace closed in June 1988 and reopened under the care of the Everyman Theatre Company in 1990, being refurbished for its one-hundredth anniversary in 1997.

The Savoy cinema on St Patrick's Street opened on 12 May 1932 and was the number one cinema for over 40 years. It could hold over 2,200 people and was the largest cinema in the city. Like the Adelphi in Dublin, the cinema was also used for concerts and in the 1960s some of the names that played there were: Tom Jones, the Bee Gees and The Rolling Stones. The biggest attraction was not a rockstar, however, but *Mary Poppins*, which opened in August 1965. Over 50,000 people came to see it in the first two weeks; almost half the population of the city.

Both the Cork International Choral Festival and the internationally renowned Cork Film Festival are legacies of An Tostal, a national spring festivity, which goes back to the 1950s. In 1956, a Waterford man, Dermot Breen, recognised the attraction of film in the arts and started the Cork Film International in 1956 at the Savoy. The first film screened was *A Town Like Alice*. Breen would later become the Irish Film Censor in 1972. Before his appointment, censors needed no background in film and were appointed from the civil service.

The Coliseum Cinema, which was a custom-built cinema, opened on 9 September 1913 on MacCurtain Street/Brian Boru Street. Before the 'talkies' were introduced in this cinema a group of men stood at the sides, popping bags and banging cans and so on to help the film along. The cinema's design was based on the tomb of Egyptian King Tutankhamun; apt, since the cinema was renowned for showing second run films known as 'resurrections'. What contributed to its closure is even more bizarre. The bus stop right outside the Coliseum doors, the stop which catered for residents of Mayfield, was moved by CIE in the early 1960s farther back on MacCurtain Street and placed outside the Metropole Hotel, next to the Palace cinema. The Coliseum closed in March 1964. Now that's Cork.

With its catchphrase 'You can rely on the Lee' the Lee cinema opened in November 1920 on Winthrop Street, only to be burned down six weeks later when the Black and Tans ravaged the city. It opened again in 1921 and was determined to be reliable, screening its first 'talkie' in December 1929, *On with the Show*. It closed for good in August 1989.

The Ritz on Washington Street did not fair much better. Reputed to be as a literal fleapit in the 1930s, ushers would pour Jeyes Fluid around the auditorium before the show. On 28 January 1938, in typical Cork fashion, the cinema went on fire. It was reopened in 1939 but closed for good on 10 August 1989 with the film – oh dear – *Mississippi Burning*.

Apart from the proliferation of multiplexes in Cork, which contributed to the demise of the smaller cinemas, the Kino arthouse cinema was established in 1996, and is to date the only independent cinema in Ireland.

Two well-known actors made Cork (though not Cork city) their home over the years. A small parish of only 570 souls, Churchtown in north Cork was where actor Oliver Reed lived out the last years of his life dying in 1999 in Malta following a drinking binge. He was well loved in the community, helping with local charities and raising £90,000 for the daughter of a local family who was physically impaired at birth. Reed starred in more than 50 films and will be remembered best for his roles in *Women in Love* and *Oliver*. On 5 May Reed was buried beneath a beech tree at Churchtown Cemetery, not far from his favourite pub, O'Brien's.

Actor Brian Dennehy, whose father emigrated from Millstreet to the US, once lived in Cork but left because – have a guess – the climate was too bad. Specifically, he said it was too damp for his son who was an asthma sufferer. With Cork being one of the wettest counties, he made a bad choice. His reasons for coming in the first place? 'Where I live there are 2,000 sheep, 65 people and three pubs. The roads are so narrow it's difficult for a donkey cart to negotiate and I hope it always stays that way.'

It runs in the blood –
food and drink in Cork

By 1713 Cork was described, rather anomalously, as 'an ambitious but ugly metropolis of 25-30,000 inhabitants ... thriving beyond all other Irish ports'. Whether it was ugly or not, its economy had expanded greatly and trade between Britain and Europe increased, as well as that between the new European colonies in North America and the West Indies. An idea of how great a port Cork became can be gained from the export figures. In 1720, 58,916 barrels of salted beef were exported from Cork; 73,108 in 1741 and 118,306 in 1744, giving Cork a name as the 'slaughterhouse of Ireland'. After beef, salted butter was the most important export and Cork was responsible for half of Ireland's total butter export in the 1740s – 71,485 cwt in 1720; 97,852 in 1744. By 1800, Cork had become the busiest transatlantic port in operation and, as its reputation suggested, also possessed the largest 'shambles' or slaughterhouse in Ireland. It exported 80 per cent of all Irish beef – approximately 22,500 tons going to America.

Charles Smith wrote what was probably the first documented history of Cork, *The History of the City and County of Cork,* in 1750 and in it said that the number of cattle slaughtered was 80,000 annually. Smith also believed in a conspiracy of sorts, saying there was another sort of beef called 'French beef' which came from the older cows and in time of peace was sold to the French. 'No wonder sailors fed with this kind of meat can't face our honest English tars, who have so much better and more substantial food in their bellies'.

Normally the whole beef, about 400lbs, was salted down into two barrels. Literally every part of the poor animal was put to some use. Tongues were barrelled and salted for the ships' officers. A by-product of beef processing was also tallow, used to make candles and soap, and 12,462 cwt was exported in 1720, a figure that increased to 18,852 cwt in 1745. Much of it was exported to Holland and Bristol. Hooves were used to make glue and oil. Hair was used in plasterwork. Heads and kidneys were sold to the poor until a way was found to ground them to be sold as 'a type of meat'; some sort of horrendous burger probably. Heart, lungs and livers were salted and sent to Scotland (what culinary tastes did the Scots have, one wonders?). The round gut was salted and sent to Venice to make skins for Bologna sausage and the small gut was made into catgut, finding its way onto musical instruments. As well as tallow, the Dutch took the shank bones; the small bones were used to make crucibles for extracting silver from lead. The blood was fed to the pigs. Last but not least, the bladder was used for to make a football. Oh, and the effluvia on the streets and slaughterhouses was spread on the land as fertiliser. Cork manure was reputed to be of the richest kind, and in the city you could buy 'slaughter dung' for 8d (3p) a horse load. The poor animals.

So what exactly is 'drisheen', the dish of Cork? To make this horror, those responsible would go to the slaughterhouses and take the blood from both the sheep (and the pigs) as well as the innards of the sheep. The oesophagus would be turned inside out and a funnel inserted in one end and filled with blood and 'other ingredients' – anything from ground bone, colon, rectum, herbs, the lot. A sturdy knot was tied at both ends and this grotesque, sock-like thing was then boiled. Drisheen is white, while black pudding, using pig's blood, is black.

At the milk market in the city, milk was sold according to use and texture – boiling milk, crackling milk and ropey milk.

'What's for dinner, ma?' 'Blood sausage and a pint of ropey milk. Now eat up!'

To help preserve butter for transportation, the casks, or firkins, were sealed with strips of dried iris that grew in the marina towards Blackpool, the hub of the cooperage trade in Cork. When the plant was dried out, the leaves were split and were waxy in texture and could be used as a sealant. The word *firkin* is the Danish for quarter barrel, representing nine gallons of butter, or 80lbs. In former days, the firkins were weighed on a large balance known as a crane. (Thus the name of the Firkin Crane cultural centre; it has nothing to do with the cranes that litter the horizon of contemporary Cork.) The butter was packed into firkins and graded. Cork had six grades – one to six – and the lowest was known blasphemously as the 'bishop'. Cork butter was shipped everywhere and there is a story that the famous explorer Stanley was said to have found a Cork firkin in the depths of Africa. With any luck he had some bread with him at the time.

Cork butter dominated the world butter trade as it entered the nineteenth century, but it began to decline slowly in the 1850s. Portugal, for example, was Cork's largest market, with 80,000 firkins imported in 1840. But by 1852 this number was reduced to 16,000, with heavy duties imposed by the Portuguese Government to stimulate local produce. Markets were also lost in the Americas and across Western Europe. The temptation to abuse the previously rigid quality control system set in. Casks were soaked in water to increase their weight and inspectors were bribed. Once the water had evaporated en route, the butter became like sponge and Cork's butter eventually gained a reputation as being inferior. By the 1870s, butter substitutes had entered the mainland European market, margarine or 'butterine' being more affordable to the working classes. On the other end of the scale, living standards also improved towards the end of the century and better quality butter, with not such a high salt content, was demanded. With Cork butter needing anything up to six pounds of salt a barrel it was considered too salty. Between 1877 and 1891 exports of butter fell from 435,000 to 170,000 firkins. The Butter Exchange in Shandon closed in 1924. Just to make sure, Cork's old enemy, fire, got hold of it in 1976. In 1984 the building opened as a heritage centre.

*Y*ou could apparently tell which side of Cork a man came from by the stout he ordered – Beamish for the southsiders, Murphy's for the northsiders. And drink at the turn of the twentieth century was considered expensive, especially whiskey. There was a story of one man who was fond of stout but never had any money. Apparently he would cross the river to the Beamish brewery and, with the help of two pint glasses, drink the slops coming out of the drain pipe into the river. With the brewery being on the southside, and given that the story tells us he 'crossed' the river, he must have been a Northsider who preferred the Beamish but was afraid of being caught.

The expense of drink for many people also comes out in a joke about the tourist in the Cork pub who is asked:

'You're a stranger here, aren't you?'

'Yes,' says the tourist, 'how did you know?'

'You took your hand off the glass.'

There were 30 brewers in Cork in 1791. Beamish & Crawford was established in 1792 with the partnership of Richard Henrick Beamish and Arthur Frederick Sharman Crawford when they acquired the Cork Porter Brewery, then owned by Edward Allen who had established the business in 1715. It was Ireland's largest brewery until 1833 and the third largest in the British Isles until 1805. In 1809, ten million gallons of porter were brewed in Cork, five million of these by Beamish. Beamish was keeping one-eighth of Cork in wages by 1834 and brewing and distilling were the exceptions to the decline of other industries in Cork. But by the end of 1836 things were not so good for the drinks industry. A protest meeting of publicans took place on 15 November 1836 in response to unusual legislation that forbade the selling of spirits between 9pm on Sunday nights and 7am the following morning. They also believed the recently established Total Abstinence Association was a 'heresy imported from abroad, unnatural in itself, and repugnant to the best traditions of Irish hospitality'. I love the way they described being abstemious as unnatural. But that's Cork.

As bad as things were that year, they were only getting started. In February 1838, Father Theobald Mathew became the leader, with gusto, of the Temperance Movement. His aim was to help the poor of Cork and alleviate their general sufferings, which were in particular caused by alcohol. By the end of that year he had enrolled an incredible 156,000 people, a figure which by January 1839 had increased to 200,000. Things were so bad for publicans that many had turned to coffee shops and by 1853 only two distilleries survived.

A brewery that saw troubled times in Cork was Murphy's, the internationally renowned stout. James J. Murphy was born in 1825 and was involved in running the successful Midleton

Distillery, in east Cork, founded by his relatives two generations earlier. Murphy sold his Midleton shares and established a brewery on a site known as Lady's Well, famous for its water which had been used by locals for generations. Before Murphy's death in 1897, the brewery was turning out 100,000 barrels of stout a year and James J. had become one of the most prosperous men in Cork. The records show that in 1881 his share of the net profits was £11,250.

Murphy also held a directorship on the board of the then Munster Bank which, in 1885, was facing closure. Murphy came to the rescue and founded a new bank, known as Munster & Leinster, thus saving the bank and becoming the pride of Cork. The bank would later merge, in 1966, with two other banking institutions – the Provincial Bank, founded in 1825 and The Royal Bank, founded in 1836 – to form AIB (Allied Irish Bank), but would continue its association with the brewery which by the 1970s was in serious financial difficulty. By 1982, AIB was left with no option but to put the business into receivership. The wheel had indeed come full circle. In 1983, however, there was better news. Heineken, the Dutch brewers (what would Cork do without the Dutch?) took over the business and saved the famous stout. After a Corkman was at the helm for a decade, Marien Kakebeeke, a Dutchman, took over in 1993. And as if that didn't hurt Cork pride enough, former Kerry footballer, Pádraic Liston, got the top job in 1998.

Sir Walter Raleigh is said to have had his first smoke in Cork at Tivoli House, where he lived for some time. He came to Cork in 1579 and used the city as a base to have a crack at the rebels – the McCarthys, Desmonds, Roches and Barrys. As well as fighting, he wrote love letters to Queen Elizabeth I (who was old enough to have been his grandmother). The letters paid off, however, because he was granted 36,000 acres of land in Cork and Waterford, making Myrtle Grove in Youghal his home until 1602, even becoming mayor of the town for a period. The people of Youghal claim it was there he had his first smoke and not in Cork. It is also believed that Raleigh, as well as bringing tobacco back to Europe (it was his men, not him, because he never travelled to that part of America himself) also brought the potato from South America, planting the first one in Ireland. After a fling with one of the Queen's maids, Raleigh was thrown into the Tower of London and in 1602 was forced to sell his land in Cork to Richard Boyle, father of Robert Boyle, the scientist responsible for Boyle's Law. Things went from bad to worse when

James I came to the throne in 1603 and Raleigh was back in the Tower for good, framed for a plot against the king. Whatever about the first smoke, he had his last one, sadly, in Whitehall, London where he was executed in October 1618.

In 1569, Cork was named as one of a small number of ports in Ireland allowed to import wine, a major advantage for the city commercially. By 1614, Cork was Ireland's premier port for the importation of wine and almost all the wine came from French ports. Whiskey however, would prove far more successful for the city. The first distillery – seemingly a very minor one – belonged to Dominic Roche in 1618, at Tobin Street where the Triskel Arts Centre now is. Commercially, however, between 1789 and 1796 three major distilleries and five more minor ones were established in Cork, comprising one-third of Ireland's distilling capacity. In 1835, Cork distillers were producing 1,400,000 gallons of whiskey annually.

The house at the junction of the North Mall and Wise's Hill was the residence of the distiller Francis Wise, after whose family the hill is named. The North Mall distillery was established on Reilly's Marsh around 1779, and by 1802 the Wise brothers were running the firm. By the 1840s their annual output was 510,000 gallons of whiskey a year. It was bought by Cork Distilleries Co. Ltd in 1866 and the main competitor was at the time Powers' Whiskey. To try and gain the upper hand, a new brand in bottles was introduced called Cork Distilleries Company Old Irish Whiskey. In the 1920s, a salesman for Cork Distilleries, Paddy Flaherty, became a great success; partly through his supposed generosity when he arrived in pubs in various towns and bought drinks for the locals. The whiskey began to sell so well that the distillery would be contacted for orders even before the arrival of the salesman, and because of the charisma of Flaherty, the whiskey was referred to in the pubs simply as Paddy Flaherty's whiskey. (It was a lot easier than asking for a shot of Cork Distilleries Company Old Irish Whiskey.) Eventually the name Paddy Flaherty appeared on the foot of the label of the bottle, and finally that was changed to Paddy, the now famous Irish whiskey. The company made gin in 1947 (Cork Dry Gin) and merged with Jameson and Powers in 1966.

Footballs, cricket balls, canon balls and oddballs – sport and its varieties in Cork

The Dutch connection just won't go away in Cork and it rears its head again with one of the city's most popular sports – road bowling. There is no substantial evidence as to how this game got to Ireland but one theory is that the Dutch soldiers introduced it when William of Orange came to Ireland in 1689. A style of bowling called 'Moors bowling' is popular in Holland still, and in 1969, the first international bowling championships were held in Losser, the Netherlands, in three disciplines – Irish Road Bowling, Dutch Moors Bowling and German Lofting. Another suggestion is that the game was introduced from Yorkshire by linen workers; it used to be played regularly in the north of England and bowling has – apparently – always been a traditional game for weavers. Another theory is that the Irish were always robbing English cannon balls, rolling them down hills or as far away as possible on open roads, and that this simplest of pleasures developed into a popular pastime. Although the sport earned some popularity in the eighteenth and nineteenth centuries in Ireland, now the game is played primarily in Cork and Armagh and some neighbouring counties.

Road bowling is played with a ball that weighs 28 oz (793.8 grams), a solid iron bowl (ball) with a circumference of approximately 18cm. Sixteen ounces is used in junior games, but Michael Collins as a youth supposedly used a 24-ounce ball to build towards the 28-ounce faster. Two contestants throw the bowl over a distance of normal roadway and the winner is the player to reach the finishing line in the least number of throws, or shots. Course distances vary in accordance with the nature of the contest; nowadays distances are usually around 4km in length. Bowling courses exist in Armagh and Cork and also some in Mayo (Castlebar), Limerick, Waterford and Louth. Despite the popularity of the sport in Cork for over 200 years, it was never popular with the English authorities (probably because they suspected the Irish had been using their cannonballs) and many bowl players appeared before the courts facing fines and possible jail sentences; fines were being dished out right up to the early 1950s.

*A*nother game that exasperated the authorities was hurling and in 1631 an order was issued in Cork city that forbade the playing of the game:

> Whereas there hath been in former times used in this City a very barbarous and uncivil kind of sport upon Easter Tuesdays, May Days, Whitson Tuesday, tossing of great balls, and hurling in the open streets with the small ball, great mischiefs have sometimes happened, as the death of men, and many wounded and maimed in these sports, said tossing and hurling in the street shall not be used the days aforesaid, nor any other, upon pain of 40s.

The game was obviously considered odd, and Arthur Young, writing 100 years later, did his best to describe it, associating the natives' love of the sport with their diet.

> Hurling is a sort of cricket, but instead of throwing the ball to knock down a wicket, the aim is to pass it through a bent stick, the ends stuck in the ground. In these matches they perform such feats of activity as ought to evidence the food they live on to be far from deficient in nourishment.

As with any county in Ireland, an amicable rivalry – particularly in sport – exists between one county and its neighbours; the city population and the rural population; and within the city, the south-side and northside. The rural population of County Cork have been charmingly described by Cork actor Niall Toibín as 'Kerrymen with shoes'. But there is a good story that shows the degree to which some people in Cork will take the north and Southside hostility. After a match between the north and south sides of the city and their respective hurling teams, Glen Rovers and St Finbarr's, two Glen supporters were making their way home after being beaten by 'De Barrs'. They stopped on the South Gate Bridge and began tossing pieces of their sandwiches to the swans, having little appetite after losing the game. Suddenly one of them asks where they were.

'On the South Gate,' he's told.

'Jesus, come out of that. We'll go up to the North Gate and feed our own feckin' swans.'

Now that's Cork.

Although banned in the 1800s, cock fighting in Cork was hugely popular and very prevalent on the northside of the city in particular. The animals, how-ever, seemed to be about the closest thing to Frankenstein's monster of the animal world that could possibly be achieved. To get the best fighting cock, they mated a bantam cock with a pheasant. A bantam cock, popular in Western Europe, was described as a 'small and aggressive rooster', or in the *Dictionary of Phrase and Fable*, popular in the 1870s, as:

> A little plucky fellow that will not be bullied by a person bigger than himself. The bantam cock will encounter a dunghill cock five times his own weight, and is there-fore said to 'have a great soul in a little body'. The bantam originally came from Bantam, in Java.

Imagine the belligerent soul of a rooster with an Indonesian twist, trapped inside the body of a pheasant and let loose on the hills of northside Cork? As if this monster was not lethal enough, the cocks practised using little leather balls over the spurs as boxing gloves, but for the fight, steel spurs were placed over the natural ones, giving them razor sharp weapons about three inches long.

Another bird that Corkonians were fond of was the pigeon. A lot of people kept pigeons in their yards, particularly in the corporation houses, even though it was actually forbidden to have pigeons in such houses. Pigeon racing, known as the 'the working man's horseracing', was both popular and well organised from the 1880s in Cork and by the 1920s the Cork Homing Union were trying to organise races from various points in Scotland. A good story relates the problems that arose from trying to keep pigeons in the yards of confined neighbourhoods. During one race, a pigeon would not land and flew in circles around the owner's home. The man then realised it was the red bloomers on the line of the woman next door that was causing the problem. When the woman eventually came out into her yard the man said 'Excuse me, do you mind taking down your drawers? I want to get my pigeon in.'

'Feck off,' she said. 'I only came out for the coal.'

Poultry was not the only animal family that Cork citizens amused themselves with. On 11 June 1770 it was recorded that the citizens of Cork took a bull in the northside, drove him through the city and 'baited him' in the southside for several hours. The bull was chased back into the city where it 'frightened four pregnant women into fits, tossed a horse nearly as high as a signpost, threw a decrepit beggar and a standing of stockings into the kennel'. Later that year it was written in a local newspaper that 'The lovers of humanity and justice wish that some method be taken to prevent the savage amusement of bull-baiting, particularly in a city so much resorted to by foreigners who must look on us as an uncivilised people, devoid of humanity'.

Cork can claim to have the third oldest cricket club in Ireland, the Cork Cricket Club founded in

1849; in 1874 County was added to the name.

However, the oldest yacht club in the world was founded in Cork. In the early 1600s, sailing as a pastime – apart from trade and defence – became popular in the Netherlands (the word 'yacht' is derived from the Dutch word *Jaghen,* meaning to hunt or chase). When King Charles II of England was in exile in the Netherlands, he was said to have grown fond of the sport. In 1660, after he was restored to the English crown, Charles was presented with a yacht called *Mary* by the Dutch and several of his courtiers, including one Murrough O'Brien (known as 'Murrough of the burnings' for his activities in Ireland during the 1641 rebellion, a title which cannot have made him popular in Cork) who had attended the court of King Charles from 1660 to 1662 and had also been created 1st Earl of Inchiquin by Charles in 1664. It is through O'Brien's influence that sailing became popular in Cork and in 1720, O'Brien's great-grandson, William O'Brien, the 9th Lord Inchiquin, and five of his friends got together and established 'The Water Club of the Harbour of Cork', known today as the Royal Cork Yacht Club. They based themselves in a Castle on Hawlbowline Island in the harbour of Cork, which was under Lord Inchiquin. In 1966 the Royal Cork and the Royal Munster Yacht Clubs agreed to merge and the Royal Cork moved to its present premises in Crosshaven, assuming the title 'The Royal Cork Yacht Club, incorporating the Royal Munster Yacht Club'.

The oldest documented steeplechase race took place in 1752 in Mallow, County Cork, when two horseman named O'Callaghan and Blake decided to race the four and a half miles between Buttevant church and St Mary's church in north Cork. Churches made good landmarks for such races because of their prominent steeples, and the sport, 'chasing from steeple to steeple', was born; otherwise known as the steeplechase. The cross-country races spread to England in 1792, where they eventually migrated from the countryside to the racetracks and became an official sport.

The first soccer team in Cork city was founded in the Alexandra Barracks, now called Collins Barracks, originally the seat of British Imperialism in the south of Ireland. The barracks were finished in 1806 and occupied by almost 2,000 men and over 150 officers. The team was called Barrackton and they were all initially British. Their great rivals were St Vincents, now a GAA club; being republican, interesting games were played. It was reported that at one match a Barrackton forward had only the goalkeeper to beat and was about to shoot when a Vincents' supporter, terrified at the prospect of a goal, drew a gun and shot the ball before the Barrackton player had time to strike.

In American baseball only four baseball pitchers in its history were ambidextrous, the first being Corkman Tony Mullane, who threw the ball both left and right handed in the same game to confuse opponents. Between 1881 and 1894, he was the best pitcher in American baseball's major leagues, winning a total of 285 games, which still puts him among the top 25 players of all time.

In 1936 the Carrigrohane circuit at Cork hosted its first motor race, an event which was repeated in 1937 and became the Cork Grand Prix in 1938. This race was the only race to be held in Ireland to the International Formula. It was also the final race on the circuit. Among the more colourful characters who took part was Prince Bira of Siam. He participated in the 1936 and '37 races but failed to finish. In 1938, however, he came second. The grand-father of the prince, whose full name was – wait for it – Birabongse Bhanutej Bhanubandh's, was portrayed in the musical comedy *The King and I*. Bira was educated in England, where he died on the London underground after suffering a heart attack in 1985.

(W)hile Cork sportsmen and women such as Christy Ring, Roy Keane, Denis Irwin and Sonia O'Sullivan have gone into the history books, others deserve a mention for achievements other than sporting. Tuckey's *Remembrancer* records a labouring man who died in the eighteenth century at the age of 127 and was said to have been able to walk 'without the help of stick or crutch, could see without spectacles, retained his senses and appetite to the last, and was followed to the grave by his descendants to the seventh generation'. On 22 June 1799 a man named Kidney died at the age of 150. He was said to have remembered that Blarney Lane was a forest and connected with Dunscombe's Wood.

The prize goes to the story of the Corkman who had reached 120 and was interviewed by a local paper.

'To what do you attribute your great age?' he was asked.

'To the fact that it is so long since I was born,' he replied.

'Seriously,' he was asked again.

'Vitamin pills,' he replied. 'I've been taking them every day since I was 110.'

A real oddball, or 'Corkscrew', recorded by Tuckey was Abraham Abell, born in 1783 and died 12 February 1851. He was born into a Quaker family and was a businessman and highly regarded philanthropist. He was also founder member of the Literary and Scientific Society and treasurer of Cork Library. He liked to walk a mile for every year of his life on his birthday. His last attempt was to walk to Youghal and back on his fifty-ninth birthday. To overcome his fear of the supernatural he slept between two skeletons for two weeks. He worked late and to remain awake he stood at his desk, sometimes on one foot.

Throwing the dart was an ancient ceremony performed triennially in Cork to mark the municipal jurisdiction over the port. A golden-headed javelin was thrown into the sea as a symbol of the Mayor's authority. The custom is believed to have originated with the Danes. The Mayor went out in a boat with officers of the corporation, and, judging by photographs of the occasion, it was a wholly male-dominated affair. It is likely that many Cork citizens were unmoved by the event. On the occasion of 22 August 1848, the corporation and the mayor together with twenty guests embarked on the steamer *Royal Alice* at Lapp's Quay, watched by a very resentful crowd, together with workers who were employed on the construction of the new wall. They all refused to applaud as was the tradition. The 'dart party', following the event, went on for a champagne dinner with officers from the Royal Fleet at Haulbowline, where toasts to the Royal Family were made. Little wonder the crowd were resentful. In the year of 1848 the country was in the grip of the Famine.

Finally, a competition of a different kind was common in Cork, according to street lore. There was a corner near the North Chapel (St Mary's and St Anne's Catholic cathedral) where supposedly in the middle of the nineteenth century they had a competition, with a prize cup, for the greatest lies and tall stories told. And some of them were good. One entrant claimed he had done over 50 miles an hour on his bicycle. When asked how he knew he had done such a thing, he said he had overtaken a motorcar, and as he passed he looked in and the speedometer in the car read 50. Another man said he was working on one of the largest boats in the country. How huge? When he was asked to climb the mast and attach the flag, by the time he got down the boat was gone. Another man, reminiscing on his poverty-stricken days as a child, claimed all his clothes were bought for him in army surplus stores. 'I went to school dressed as a Japanese Admiral,' he said.

Mind your slanguage

Two touring Englishmen in 1748 reported that the people of Cork had no recognisable accent, which meant that either it was unique or that there was such a great mix of nationalities present then that there was no defining a Cork accent. We know now, of course, that the Cork accent is very unique. Apart from the accent however, there is also the Cork slang. Hiberno-English, (from *Hibernia*, the Latin word for Ireland) the vocabulary of which is not in use in British English today but is still in use in Ireland (although on the decline) would be one obvious place to look for a source. And the strong English presence in tight-knit Cork would have meant that a substantial number of Irish words were assimilated into the English spoken there. Hiberno-English applies not only to 'loan' words that were used directly such as 'ommadhawn' for a fool from the Irish *amhadán*, but also to how words were pronounced, as in *meejum* for 'medium' or *fillum* for 'film'. Then there was the influence of the Nordic language, the more limited introduction of words from Hindustani courtesy of the Munster Fusiliers. There was also the Shelta language, the language of Irish Travellers, a distinct ethnic group that used to be referred to as 'tinkers' from the Irish words *ceard* meaning 'smith' (as in tinceard, tin-smith) or according to another source, from the Middle English 'tynekere', both referring to their occupation. And there is, of course, the language whose origins are 'unknown' on Cork's streets. The latter is claimed as Cork's very own.

Cork historian and writer Sean Beecher offered this passage as an illustration of Cork slang:

Whacker Murphy went shifting in the Arc and clocked a dolly from the Gurrane. She was a lasher with a pair of josies that would act as buffers for the *Innisfallen*. He took her for a jorum. She started on whackers, but changed to meejums. He was on half ones. On the way home, they went up Bob and Joan's, and he got a great stall. He made a jag for the Statue, even though he thought he'd get fifty.

Translation
Whacker Murphy went chasing girls in the Arcadia Ballroom and met up with a girl from Gurranbraher. She was a very nice girl with a great pair of breasts

that would have acted as buffers for the *Innisfallen* ship. He took her for a drink. She started on small brandies but changed to half-pints. He was on half whiskies. On the way home, he got a great bit of sex at Bob and Joan's [well-known statues of two Cork orphans]. He made a date for the Statue but believed that she would never show up.

The following are some examples of Cork slang (some of the words are not unique to Cork) to illustrate the diversity of its origins.

Bate. This means a piece of bread or a sandwich and Beecher suggests it is a good example of old Norse language entering general usage, with 'bate' stemming from the word *beita* to bite. The word appears to be used in Cork only.

Bazz. Used in Cork to refer to female pubic hair, but there is a reference in Hiberno-English to the word 'bazz' referring to a few day's beard growth. A 'bazzer' was also used in Cork to refer to a haircut, and there was a barber's on Washington Street called 'Bazzers'. The word does a have a certain ring to it: 'I'm going to get a bazzer'. A female saying it however, does not sound quite so charming.

Boodawn. Over to the males now, and this word is used for an erection. There does not appear to be any other similar words from Hiberno-English, so we can assume that Cork lads are unique in this matter. The only word in general old Irish slang that is close to it is the word 'bookeran' (from the Irish word *bóichreán*) meaning dried cow dung. But that's not very flattering for the Cork lads, is it? The word 'Connihaly' is used in Cork – and only Cork by the looks of it – for a small penis and no other explanation is given for its widespread use only that it comes from a man named Connie Healy, who lived in Cork and had a small penis. God bless the man's family.

Chats. Meaning breasts in Cork slang. But the word has also been used in Irish slang to refer to a small, inferior potato, which does not really flatter Cork women unfortunately. It is even less flattering to know that the word was also used in Irish slang to refer to the cheap methylated spirits drunk by alcoholics.

Collops. Another quite derogatory term used to refer to a woman's legs, specifically the calves. The word comes from the Irish *colpa* and is actually a unit of measure of grazing land for cattle or sheep. However, the Irish word *colpach* means a heifer, and it is probably from this that the word derives its meaning.

Crubeens. This word is of Irish origin, but it is still

used in Cork. It comes from the Irish word *crúb*, meaning hoof or claw, giving the word *crúibín*. The term now specifically refers to pigs' feet, or trotters, which were supposed to have been a delicacy in Cork, particularly after the pub.

Drisheen. This is the word for Cork tripe (see food and drink section), a type of blood sausage. It comes from the Irish *drisín,* meaning an animal's intestine. Another word that is close to it and makes it even less appealing is the slang word, probably Scottish in origin, 'drizzen' meaning a moaning sound made by a cow.

Langer. This word has been adopted by the Corkonians and was even the title of a recent song by Tim O'Riordan and Natural Gas.

The word can mean an eejit and it can also refer to a penis. Both can be used as terms of abuse and, unless there are two different ways of saying the word, it is up to the abused to ascertain what exactly he is being called – a penis, or an eejit. Sean Beecher alludes to the 'langur' in attempting to trace the origins of this word, the 'langur' being a long-tailed monkey from India. But that is probably just Corkmen showing off. Longar, according to another source, means 'to sway' in Irish from which we get another word, 'langered', which means drunk. So a 'langered langer' must be some spectacle in Cork. Just to clear things up, Roy did not actually call Mick a 'langer' on that fateful day in Saipan in 2002. We can quote what he did say just to demonstrate further the use of language in Cork:

> Who the f**k do you think you are, having meetings about me? You were a crap player, you are a crap manager. The only reason I have any dealings with you is that somehow you are manager of my country and you're not even Irish, you English c**t. You can stick it up your bo**ix.

Mebs. This word is used to refer to small potatoes and marbles and also in Cork, to testicles. So anything small and round presumably. The origin of the word is unknown, but there are other references to the word being used elsewhere in Ireland to refer to small marbles, with 'taws', the word for large marbles. In Ulster, however, the word 'taw' is reserved for testicles only. 'Taws' in Ulster, 'Mebs' in Cork. What might that tell us then?

Meejum. A 'meejum' refers to a half-measure of stout, or a half pint. The likelihood is that it comes from the word 'medium', as Beecher pointed out and is an example of a Hiberno-English word with a corrupted pronunciation. The measure had no actual standard and the quantity probably depended on the pourer. It was very popular about 50 years ago in Cork. As opposed to a small measure, the word 'jorum' refers to an alcoholic drink, usually a large measure, the word 'jorum' meaning a large drinking vessel. As for the origins of the word, nobody seems to know.

A *noodeenaw* is a term for an annoying person in Cork, and a 'noodenaddy' is the term for an indecisive or dithering person in County Kerry. Both would come from the Irish *niúidí neáidí*, meaning hesitant in speech or manner, so we will have to give that one to the Kerrymen.

Pawny is a good example of a word introduced by the Munster Fusiliers. The Royal Munster Fusiliers was one of the most famous Irish regiments of the British Army. It consisted of five battalions, the first two being the 101st and the 104th with a lineage that stretched back to India in the eighteenth century. There were also three militia battalions – South Cork Militia, Kerry Militia and Limerick Militia. The 101st was formed in 1759 and consisted of three companies of the East India Company's Bombay European Regiment. The 104th formed in

1760 as the King's Volunteers, then became the 104th Bengal Fusiliers. Both were eventually absorbed into the Royal Munster Fusiliers. The regiment saw much overseas service in India and fought also in the First World War in France, Gallipoli, Salonica and Egypt. Four members won Victoria crosses. The word 'pawny' was used in Cork for rain and is from the Hindustani *pani* for water.

Scauld: tea. A good cup of scauld or scauldy is fairly widespread in Ireland and not exclusive to Cork. It comes from the Irish word scall to burn or scald. Although the term is used now to refer to tea, an earlier reference to scalteen, with the same root, refers to a specific drink made by boiling a mix of whiskey, water, sugar, butter and pepper.

Skelp: means a blow, or strike, particularly with an open hand. A confusing word, but one source mentions 'one gets a skelp on the pus (face) and a slap on the jaw'. Nice to know what you're going to get if you have a scrap in Cork.

Soolach: meaning dirty, soapy water or effluence and it is thought to be taken from the Irish word *súlach* meaning juice or gravy. There was also the use of the word 'soorlucking' in Kerry – which will give Corkonians a bit of a laugh. The word means actually looking in dirty water – presumably farm-yard muck – for food.

Steamer: used to refer to a cigarette and is one example of a Shelta word, *stima*, meaning a tobacco pipe. There is also a word of Scottish/Nordic origin, 'stim', meaning a glimmer.

Tráwneen: an object/person of little value or importance. Beecher points to the Irish word *tráithnín*, meaning a strong blade of grass, in tracing the origins of this word. There is also the word 'thraw' old English for misery or calamity, a likelier derivation.

Immigrants, emigrants and freemen of Cork

More than 60 years ago there were roughly 400 members in Cork's Jewish community. Now it would not even reach double figures. In the 1950s, the Jewish community in Cork numbered about 300 and had its own rabbi. By the 1970s this number had fallen to twenty and was no longer served by a rabbi. By 1998, the community, which traces its presence in Cork back to 1690, was thought to number only eight. However, under Jewish teaching, a basic unit of ten Jewish males over the age of thirteen must be present to perform a service, so the services in the synagogue, which is located on the South Terrace, no longer operate. The most prominent member of the Jewish community in Cork, Gerald Y Goldberg, a lawyer who once represented writer Frank O'Connor, died on 2 January 2004. Goldberg was lord mayor in 1977, the first member of the Jewish community to become mayor. In 1989, in Monerea in an area that was known as 'Jew Town', Bord Gais presented a piece of ground in remembrance of the Jewish community and called it Parc Shalom, or Shalom Park.

Cork has hosted a Muslim community for more than twenty years. Their numbers have steadily grown from about 500 in the 1980s to the current figure of around 1,500, according to the last chairman of the Muslim Society in Cork, Mr Karim Abdullah, although the number could be over 2,000. In 2005, no mosque exists in Cork and a hall in Togher is used.

Of approximately 5,000 Huguenots who came to Ireland after the persecutions in late seventeenth-century France, about 300 came to Cork and had established themselves by the mid-eighteenth century. They were mostly involved in the textile industry, but the most notable was Joseph Lavitt, who arrived in the 1690s and became a successful property developer. It is said that he began his enterprise selling brandy to the Williamite soldiers. But his main business became overseas trade, sugar refining and property development along the quays in Cork. Lavitt's Quay is clearly named after him and Morrison's Island was originally called Lavitt's Island. Another interesting family of Huguenots were the Gobles, silversmiths who were prominent members of the guild that incorporated gold and silversmiths. Robert and his son, also Robert, were skilled silversmiths and were in demand by churches, crafting items such as cups and plates for Christ Church and St Finbarre's. They were also responsible for the silver boxes presented to the recipients of the freedom of Cork.

The Quakers, also known as the Religious Society of Friends, have been in Cork since the 1650s. The present Quaker meeting house was opened at Summerhill South in 1939. George Fox, who founded the Quakers, had extensive properties in Cork. They were called Quakers because 'I bade them tremble at the word of the Lord', wrote Fox. Many Cork Quakers were merchants and businessmen and in the nineteenth century the Beales, the Pikes, the Newsoms, and other Quakers were among the most successful merchants and industrialists in Cork. During the Famine, the Cork Quakers, sticking to their principles of brotherly love, made great efforts to help those suffering.

William Penn (1644-1718) moved to Macroom Castle when he was twelve and after studying at Oxford, where he was a 'rebellious' student, returned to Ireland and converted to Quakerism in 1665. He was arrested in Cork on a riot charge and on his father's death, Admiral Penn, in 1670 Penn was left claims on the government worth £16,000, in lieu of which he received a grant of territory in America. From Dundanion Quay (later Navigation Wall, then King's Quay, now Monahan Road in Ballintemple) in August 1682, he sailed to the Americas and founded the state now called Pennsylvania. He proposed calling it just 'Sylvania' on account of its forests (*sylvania* being Latin for woodlands). However, King Charles II wished to have the 'Pen' prefix to honour his father. The site he chose for the capital was the junction of the Delawere and Schylkill rivers, and we called it Philadelphia, the city of brotherly love.

James Beale, Quaker, businessman and also president of the Cork School of Art and Science, chartered the steamship *Sirius* from the St George Steam Packet Company. With 450 tons of coal on board as well as 40 passengers, the ship left Cork on 3 April 1838 and arrived in New York on 22 April with Beale as captain. Unfortunately, after another crossing the ship was transferred to the cross channel route to Britain and on 16 January 1847, in heavy fog, it struck a reef near Ballycotton, County

Cork, and sank to the bottom of the ocean. The *Sirius* is claimed by Corkonians as being the first steamship to make the Atlantic crossing; a claim disputed by none other than the Dutch (ooooh!) whose steamship, the *Curacao,* crossed from Holland to the Southern Caribbean island in 1826.

Roughly only four per cent of the twelve million people who passed through Ellis Island, New York, between 1892 and 1954, when it finally closed, were Irish and the first person ever to pass through was a girl from Cork, Annie Moore. She was born on 1 January 1877 and arrived in America on 1 January 1892 with her two younger brothers. Her parents and elder brother had travelled to America three years earlier. She was presented with a special certificate at New York Harbour and a $10 gold piece. The family later moved to Indiana and then Texas, where she married a descendant of Daniel O'Connell in Waco and had eight children. Tragically, Annie Moore died when she was hit by a train in Texas in 1923. A bronze sculpture of herself and two brothers was unveiled by President Mary Robinson on 8 February 1993 at Deepwater Quay, Cobh, and later the same year a statue of her was unveiled at Ellis Island. It is the sole statue on the island.

The first Irish Catholic mayor of New York,

William R. Grace (1832-1904), was born on 10 May 1832 in the family home of Riverstown estate in north Cork. Originally working in Peru, where he began as a partner with the shipping firm of John Bryce at Callao, he later founded W.R. Grace and Company in New York in 1865, which served as a front for Grace Brothers in Callao and soon had offices in San Francisco and all over the west coast of South America. When Peru built its rail system, he secured practically all the contracts for supplying the builders. He became an advisor to the government of Peru and handled the business of arming their military. He became mayor of New York in 1880 and in 1897 established the Grace Institute to give free tuition to women in a variety of practical and vocational subjects, which he founded after a study of economic conditions of workmen's families during a strike in one of his enterprises.

Born in Fermoy, John B. McDonald (1844-1911) left for America with his parents in 1847 and would become one of the country's most successful contractors. His projects include building New York's first subway; between 1868 and 1900 several companies had tried and failed. In 1904 the first phase was opened and ran from City Hall to 145th Street. He was also the contractor for Jerome Park reservoir in New York City which was, on completion, the largest in the world.

William Ford, Henry Ford's father, was born in Ballinascarthy, County Cork in 1826 and went to America in 1847. Henry Ford was born on 30 July 1863 on a farm in Michigan eight miles west of Detroit, a city that would become known as Motortown, or simply Motown. He became famous for his Model T, the car for the multitudes, in 1908, and sold 15 million in the US alone. He was the first to introduce assembly lines for cars in 1913, turning out a complete chassis in 93 minutes. In 1914 he announced he would be paying a minimum wage of $5 a day and would reduce the working day from nine hours to eight. Ford set up his first European plant in Cork, although many believe it was not for sentimental reasons. He originally approached the British government about setting up a factory in Southampton. However, at the time, February 1917, England was in the middle of the First World War and feared people would leave munitions factories to work for Ford. So he decided on Cork and the racecourse was given over for an agreed fee of £10,000. Two thousand workers were to be employed at a rate of one shilling an hour. A story about Ford in Cork says that when he was asked to donate to a local hospital, he offered a donation of £5,000. However, the announcement in the paper read 'Ford Offers £50,000 to Cork Hospital'. Seemingly tricked into giving the £50,000, he asked for a verse beside his name on the memorial: 'I was a stranger, and you took me in.'

The first mayor of Cork was Richard Wine, who became mayor in 1273. He was succeeded by the aptly named Richard Lee in 1274. The first mayoralty chain was presented to Maurice Roche in 1579 by Queen Elizabeth for his services in the rebellion of the Earl of Desmond. William Lyons was the first Catholic mayor of Cork for nearly 200 years when elected on 25 October 1848. The first Lord Mayor was Sir Daniel Hegarty in 1900, the title of Lord conferred by Queen Victoria. The first female mayor was Dublin-born Jennie Dowdall in 1959. Thomas MacCurtain, the first Republican Lord Mayor, was murdered by Crown forces in his home in Blackpool on 20 March 1920. His friend and successor, Terence MacSwiney, died on hunger strike in Brixton, London on 25 October 1920.

The freedom of the city dates from the fourteenth century, where persons become honorary burgesses of a city. But owing to the tragic fire in Cork's courthouse in 1891, when the municipal documents were destroyed, the full list of Freemen of Cork was one of the many casualties. Some notable names are, however, known. Jonathan Swift was granted the freedom of Cork on 20 January 1736, probably because of his philanthropic efforts for the native industries. However, three members of the corporation objected and Swift was not happy to hear about it. He said at the time:

> I am told ... that the city of Cork hath sent me my silver box of freedom, but I know nothing of it ... when I get my Cork box, I will certainly sell it for not being gold.

The box arrived but was sent back because it was not inscribed. Swift never warmed to the box (and possibly the idea of being a Freeman of Cork) leaving the box to a friend of his to keep tobacco in.

The Cork Corporation must have been unmoved by the Rising of 1803 leader Robert Emmet's speech from the dock, by conferring the Freedom of the City on the prosecuting attorney Hugh O'Grady. Philanthropist Andrew Carnegie, who donated £10,000 to Cork city for the building of a library was given the freedom of the city in 1902. Former presidents of the US Woodrow Wilson was conferred in 1919 and John F. Kennedy in 1963.

In 2005 Roy Keane and Sonia O'Sullivan were given the Freedom of the City. 'I felt there was a need to acknowledge the sporting culture of the city,' said Lord Mayor Sean Martin. 'Sonia has been a great ambassador, a world champion. And I felt there was a need to acknowledge the football culture of the city too. Roy is one of the greatest footballers this country has ever produced.' Much criticism was justifiably made of the fact that fellow footballer Denis Irwin was left out. The *Irish Echo* said of Irwin's exclusion, when the announcement was made in May 2005: 'The man from Togher only played 902 professional games, yet won a mere seven Premiership titles, a solitary European Cup, a trifling Cup Winners' Cup, and a meagre three FA Cups. Not to mention 56 Irish caps.' The *Echo* also bemoaned the fact that previously only two members of Cork's sporting community had been given the Freedom of the City – former GAA President and distinguished Cork hurler, Con Murphy, and six-times All-Ireland medallist and former Taoiseach Jack Lynch. Christy Ring, the greatest of them all, died without ever being celebrated in this way by Cork.

Bibliography

Beecher Sean, *Cork 365*, The Collins Press, 2005

Beecher, Sean *A Dictionary of Cork Slang*, The Collins Press 1991

Beecher, Sean, *An Gaeilge in Cork City, An Historical Perspective to 1894*, Goldy Angel Press, 1993

Beecher, Sean, *The Story of Cork*, Mercier Press, 1971

Cadogan, Tim, *Cork in Old Photographs*, Gill MacMillan, 2003

Cooke, Richard T, *The Cork Millennium Book: My Home by the Lee*, Irish Millennium Publications, 1999

Coughlan, John, *100 Cork Sporting Heroes*, Evening Echo Publications, 2003

Cussen, Paul, *Cork A Pocket Guide*, The Collins Press, 2004

Dolan, Terence Patrick, *A Dictionary of Hiberno-English*, Gill & Macmillan, 1999

Flynn, John and Kelleher, Jerry, *Cork Journeys in America*, High Table Publishing, 2003

Foley, Niall, *Uniquely Cork*, The Collins Press, 1991

Jeffries, Henry Alan, *Historical Perspectives*, Four Courts Press, 2004

Kelleher, D.L., *The Glamour of Cork*, Talbot Press Ltd, 1919

Lincoln, Colm, *Steps and Steeples*, O'Brien Press, 1980

Mac Carthy, W.G., *A Short History of Cork*, Killeen, 1996

McNamara, T.F., *Portrait of Cork*, Watermans Cork, 1981

McCarthy, Morty, *Dowtcha Boy! An Anthology of Cork Slang*, The Collins Press, 2004

MacHale, Des, *The Humour of Cork*, Mercier Press, 1995

McSweeney, John, *Cork Cinemas*, Rose Arch Publications, 2003

O'Sullivan, John L, *Cork City Gaol*, Ballyheada Press, 1996

Pettit, S.F., *My City by the Lee*, Studio Publications Cork, 1987

Pettit, Dr S.F., *The Streets of Cork*, Studio Publications 1982

Pochin Mould, Daphne D.C., *Discovering Cork*, Brandon 1991

Power, Vincent, *Voices of Cork*, Blackwater Press, 1997

Share, Bernard, *Slanguage: A Dictionary of Irish Slang*, Gill & Macmillan, 1997

St Leger, Alicia, *Silver Sails and Silk Huguenots in Cork 1685-1850*, Cork Civic Trust, 1991

Tuckey, Francis H, *Cork Remembrancer*, Osborne savage and Son, 1837

Verdon, Michael, *Shawlies, Echo Boys, The Marshes and the Lanes. Old Cork Remembered*, O'Brien Press, 1993